ROELAND BROECKAERT

SERVANT-
LEADERSHIP

TOUGH ON RESULTS
TENDER ON PEOPLE

Lannoo
Campus

This book was originally published as Dienend leidinggeven, LannooCampus, 2016.

D/2024/45/80 – ISBN 978 94 014 0726 7 – NUR 808

Design: Tripleclick Design
Photo author: Wouter Mertens
Translation: Michael Pauls

LannooCampus Publishers is a subsidiary of Lannoo Publishers, the book and multimedia division of Lannoo Publishers nv.

LannooCampus Publishers
Vaartkom 41 box 01.02   P.O. Box 23202
3000 Leuven   1100 DS Amsterdam
Belgium   The Netherlands
www.lannoocampus.com

CONTENTS

'A leader is best when people barely know he exists, when his work is done, his aim fulfilled, they will say: we did it ourselves.'

— Lao Tzu, 600 v.C.

PROLOGUE

*'Leadership is not a function or position you take,
it is a service you give.'*

— Simon Sinek, expert and author in leadership development

Do you remember what you wanted to be as a child? Maybe you
dreamed of becoming a fireman, draughtsman, accountant, lawyer,
social worker, engineer, craftsman, nurse or teacher. But manager?
Perhaps for the first few years of your career, you practised the
profession for which you initially felt a calling. Now you are leading
a team, or steering an organisation. Whether you work in advertising
or education, in production or in services, healthcare or banking: you
accomplish something and you do this together with other people.

But just as a good footballer is not necessarily a successful coach,
being a driven professional does not automatically make you an
effective manager. After all, leadership is an entirely different metier,
a profession in its own right. The other day, during the break of a
leadership programme, I heard a manager say that it was simple after
all, that you just had to make sure your employees were happy.
In essence, I agreed with him; after all, your employees are the organisation's capital strength. But is it that simple? What about the other
stakeholders around your employees: your customer or product, your
organisation and last but not least yourself?

In managing your people, you might recognise the following
challenges: you notice a tension between time and priority in your time
management. You want to delegate, but you're concerned about how it
will work with some colleagues. You notice that this makes it difficult
to let go of some executive tasks. You don't find it easy to select the
right people for vacant positions in your team. You notice that some
colleagues need clear feedback or boundaries rather than yet another

casual chat about a recurring issue. You see individual differences between the people you work with, but you also want to treat everyone as 'equal before the law'. You already have a framework for leadership in your head, but find the gap between theory and practice sometimes quite large. You do want to bring peace to your team, but often things happen that make you yourself unsettled as a manager. Often, your work is thwarted by things over which you have no direct influence: people speak to you about colleagues or expectations of the environment or organisational changes. This can create extra pressure.

You want to create a collective ambition with your people; you want to strive for a good product or excellent service and for motivated employees. This is only possible if they experience DRIVE in their jobs: if they can take on their responsibilities, if they work efficiently, if they believe in what they do support the organization's objectives, if they feel connected with each other and develop their talents. You want to be tough on results but soft on relationships. This book is about how to achieve these things in your organisation.

It aims to bridge the gap between scientific research, effective tools and the often much more complex reality. Servant-leadership helps you implement these in your own leadership, your own team or organisation. It requires a combination of obligatory choices on the one hand and gradual personal development on the other. To illustrate this, the book concludes with a case study in which Servant-Leadership was implemented in a hospital. The biggest challenge for you as a leader, at least in my view, is to get more satisfaction and enjoyment from your task. To feel good and comfortable in this role, I think it is crucial to deepen your own vision of leadership. That way, you can best influence your employees, the organisation as a whole, the stakeholders and yourself, by acting on your own values and beliefs.

I wish for you, dear reader, that your leadership may have a beneficial impact on yourself, on everyone around you and on the quality of your work together.

Philippe van der Wal
CEO Human Mobility Group

INTRODUCTION

SERVANT-LEADERSHIP

'You might obey a leader who has power and is authoritarian. You might do what he asks you to do. But you will not necessarily strive to serve him or the organisation in a way that brings out the best and most engaged version of yourself. That is, unless you and the people you work with also truly respect and appreciate the leader for who he is and what he does.'

— Dan B. Allender, professor and author of Leading with a Limp

Servant-leadership, fortunately, is not hype. Nor is it anything new. As the quote from Lao-Tzu at the front of this book illustrates, it has been around for centuries. More than that, almost everyone applies it in their daily lives. Parenting, for example, is often a form of servant-leadership. Consider your function as a parent when teaching your little son to ride a bike:

You take your son outside on a sunny day and provide a safe environment. After all, you won't let him practise on a busy brick road or a sloping street strewn with pebbles. You explain to him how cycling works, put him on the saddle and guide him the first few metres with your hand. When, after some practice, your son zig-zags his first metres, you shout at him that he is doing great. When he falls that inevitable first time, you are quick to be near him. You rub the sore knee, advise where necessary and boost his confidence.

When he falls a second time and throws his brand new bike in the street, crying, you speak to him about it. You make it clear that you understand that he is frustrated and therefore crying, that all beginnings are difficult and he will learn.

After a few weeks of practice, you decide together that the training wheels can come off. You explain to your son that he has made it all by himself so far. When you finally see him cycling up and down the street smiling, you beam with pride.

When you teach your little son to cycle, you will naturally start looking for the perfect balance between leading and serving. Of course, you have already cycled many miles yourself, so he can still learn a lot from you. But most of all, you want him to learn on his own, so that soon he will be able to go out on his own. In servant-leadership it is the same: you look for the balance between leading and serving, between limiting and giving space, between making rules and letting people discover for themselves.

Servant-leadership as a philosophy starts from the idea that as a leader, you do not create followers, but new leaders. A servant leader helps his employees develop, and teaches them to inspire others to do the same. It calls on the leader to create a working environment where his employees can unleash their talents and passion, and where they visibly contribute to the organisation's mission and goals.

The development of the employee is central, and this is because the servant leader believes that the real capital of an organization is in his employees. He wants them to succeed and be able to achieve success. After all, the success of the employees is the success of the company, or in other words, the results of an organisation are determined by the performance of its employees. For the servant leader, it is therefore of the utmost importance for his employees to flourish within his organisation.

The effectiveness of this approach can be found everywhere, especially in nature.

SERVANT-LEADERSHIP IS NATURAL

'It is the long history of humankind (and animal kind, too) those who learned to collaborate and improvise most effectively have prevailed.'

— Charles Darwin

A pack constantly pursues goals together: they search for a territory together and go hunting. They often catch animals many times larger than themselves. They depend on each other to achieve their goals and work together very effectively. Not for nothing do Indians and Inuit regard wolves as their teachers. Underlying this is the basic attitude of the pack, namely that bonding and working together for a common goal leads to better results than competition.

For a long time, biologists mistakenly assumed that a wolf pack organised itself in a rigid, hierarchical manner. At the top of the pack would be the alpha male and alpha female, below were the beta animals, below them the gamma animals and so on. Leadership would be imposed by strength, age and physical confrontation. This hypothesis is analogous to the outdated proposition that effective organisations are best served by a pyramidal structure and authoritarian leadership models to achieve good results.

In our times, however, leading biologists have shown that a wolf pack organises itself much more horizontally than is commonly assumed, rather like a family (Packard in Mech and Boitani, 2003). Wolves have strong social bonds among themselves. Thus, they decide together who will be the leader. The wolf with the greatest mental strength is chosen, not necessarily the strongest wolf, but the one who can best adapt to changing circumstances. So there is no such thing as a born 'alpha wolf'. From the leadership practices of a pack we can learn a lot about how to manage our own organisations more effectively. The leadership of the 'alpha wolf' is not based on conflict, fear or control, but rather on targeted interventions to reduce tensions in the group (Packard, in Mech and Boitani, 2007). The leader never has dictatorial control. The social structure of the pack can be compared to a democracy that relies on constant interaction. The alpha male will not 'lead for the sake of leading', but make the pack members themselves responsible for the best solutions for the whole group, without compromising the pack's social structure. During hunting, for example, wolves take over the leadership role from each other for a while from time to time. All animals in the pack have a responsibility in this. Thus, everyone contributes to the smooth functioning of the group.

Furthermore, there have been several observations of wolf behaviour that show empathy. For example, an older wolf with arthritis was not left to fend for itself, but fed by wolves that were still able to hunt. Young pups are not only fed by the parents, but by the whole pack.

The operation of a wolf pack is evidence from nature that the most effective result hardly comes from a rigid, hierarchical structure where there is no say from the members involved and where the leader dictates on a basis of threats and displays of power.

These are all things that bear a strong analogy to human social systems. But how then can a servant leader act in a 'human pack'? What basic attitude underpins natural leadership?

A MANAGER GETS THE EMPLOYEES HE (DE)SERVES

'Group members only accept the influence and guidance of a leader they believe has the means to fulfil their needs. People follow (and have their actions guided by) a leader who, they believe, will ensure they get what they want or need.'

— Thomas Gordon, communication and leadership expert

Sociological research has shown that there are no innate personality differences between leaders and non-leaders (Gordon, 2010). So be reassured that leadership potential is not something you have or do not have by nature. Yet I have noticed during various training courses that similarities regularly emerge between leaders in different sectors. People who advance to leadership are often experts who seem to be born leaders with just the right set of traits, but some pitfalls are present there too.

These types are regularly characterised by the 'three Ps': they want to perform, to perfect their skills and to please their people. Such traits do encourage these managers to take a facilitating or coaching approach. The biggest problem with these three Ps is that they do not fully empower the employee in the long run. From his desire to 'perform' or 'perfect', the manager may be less comfortable with handing over responsibilities. As a result, he may feel the urge to take over various operational tasks himself, hindering his employees' growth. When, at the same time, he clings to the hope of pleasing people, he may find it difficult - besides letting go of operational tasks - to hold people accountable, and thereby compromises results.

This book starts from the premise that leadership is most effective when the manager places as much ultimate responsibility with his employees as possible, rather than on himself. Therefore, from his awareness of the effects of the three Ps, the manager should shift his focus. The importance of this was recently highlighted in a study (Rath & Conchie, 2008) in which more than 1 million people were surveyed. Here, it was found that the main reason for job resignations was not pay, travel time or job tasks. The main reason was the way leadership was provided.

From that science, then, it seems fair to say that leadership stands or falls on group members accepting or rejecting the influence of the leader, rather than on someone being 'assigned a role' from on high. Just because someone declares you a leader does not mean you effectively are one. The real judgement on that can only be made by the people you lead. It is therefore especially important for a leader to get a mandate from his or her employees (Gordon, 2010).

So how do you acquire that mandate? Why do employees or team members accept the influence of one manager and not another? What happens during such interactions? According to the servant-leadership philosophy, you earn this mandate by finding the right balance between serving and directing. Servant-leadership, for instance, is a very common philosophy in several armies. For instance, the word 'sergeant' comes from 'servant'. On the one hand, soldiers get to know the sergeant as someone who shouts hoarsely when there is a need to drill, who gets angry when latecomers show up and asks the utmost of his men during exhausting physical trials. But at the same time, they know him as the one who is most concerned when someone suffers an injury, who waits until everyone has eaten before serving himself and who takes the lead in battle. In battle, he chooses the path he deems safest for his men and himself.

Because leadership is about what you ultimately do or do not do, you can look at leadership development as striving to be the most authentic and effective leader hidden within you. As a servant-leader, you act out of a willingness to put the needs of your team members at the centre - while always keeping an eye on the organisation's vision and goals (Gordon, 2010). Whenever you succeed in doing this, you 'deposit' resources into your colleagues' relational bank account, as it were, and build up credit. So in servant-leadership, you find out what your employees' needs are and then try to create a context in which those needs can be met. There is a constant interaction: as a leader, you only get loyal employees by being loyal to your team. A good touchstone is to lead the way you yourself want to be led. To put this into daily practice, try working according to the 'ABC' of employee needs (Pink, 2013). Your employee has a number of requirements you must consider:

- **Autonomy**: as much as possible, the employee wants to be able to decide what he does and how he does something.

- **Bonding** with a cause and the team: the employee wants to contribute to a cause – a cause that is also meaningful to him. He wants to feel connected to the team and the organisation.

- **Competence**: the employee wants to be good at something.

EXERCISE

- Consider an executive who has been an inspiration to you. Who managed to bring out the best professional version of yourself? What did that person do? What did he not do? How did this affect you? Can you make the link to the ABC?

- Think about an executive you felt a lot of loyalty towards. What did he do differently from the others? What was the effect of this? Can you link it to the ABC?

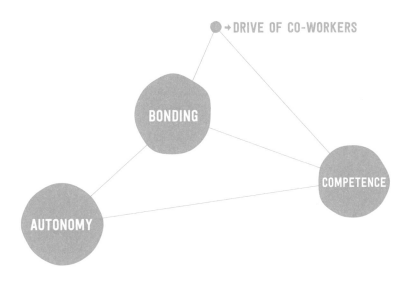

AN ORGANISATION GETS THE LEADERS IT REWARDS

'Our top-down pyramid style of management is a very old concept borrowed from centuries of war and monarchies.'

— James C. Hunter

From research on leadership among traditional populations, where a leader is unable to control the group hierarchically, we see that the leader's position is often determined by the value assigned to him by group members. Among the Kung, a hunter-gatherer people in Namibia, we read in old accounts: 'None of them is arrogant, dominant, cold or boastful.' Among the Kung, such traits make you ineligible even to become a leader. We also find that a lust for opulent lifestyles and possessions is rather less common than among the average households in the tribe.

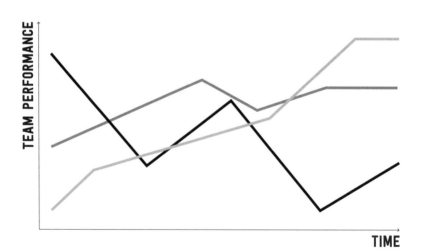

In such a context, with a limited hierarchy and the absence of large power differences, the principles of servant-leadership - as in the wolf pack - are naturally integrated. However, organisations are usually organised hierarchically, with large disparities in power. This leads to the fact that in addition to the mandate of your employees, you also need the mandate of your organisation to become a servant-leader (Van Vugt & Wildschut, 2012).

In many organisations, managers still have a hierarchical mandate: 'I am the boss because the boss says I am the boss. And after all, he is the boss.' There is nothing wrong with this initially. However, it is common for leaders to become authoritarian in this structure because they rely on the 'power' they have been assigned. It then soon happens that teams do not so much work towards results, but rather follow the will of the leader.

However, recent studies (Nuijten, 2011, pp. 98-102) show that an authoritarian approach to leadership has a negative rather than positive long-term effect. The figure shows the results of the study. The black line represents organisations with 'unclear' leadership; there, within the group itself, it was not yet clear who the leader was or what style he used. The grey line represents traditional leadership with an authoritarian focus. The blue line represents organisations where servant-leadership was applied. It can be clearly seen that this style proved most effective over time (Nuijten, 2011, pp. 98-102). This can be explained by the fact that the traditional system provokes behaviour in its employees that the organisation does not actually want. For instance, decisions are taken top-down, without much eye and ear for the experiences at the bottom of the ladder. Employees then show resistance and are unwilling or unable to cope with change. Moreover, an authoritarian or very directive leadership culture in an organisation more often leads to less vertical communication, less exchange between colleagues from different departments and more so-called 'political behaviour': sneering, gossiping, minimum commitment (only doing what has to be done), covering up mistakes and glossing over disappointing results.

Rivalry also develops among colleagues to gain favour with the manager, a process that can be very destructive for the team.

It is my personal belief that very many recent illnesses can be directly or indirectly linked to this way of working. In Belgium, the cost of long-term illnesses such as depression and burnout has recently exceeded that of unemployment benefits. The Dutch Centraal Bureau voor de Statistiek, in turn, states that as much as 2.2 billion of GNP goes to long-term absenteeism, which would amount to 25,000 euros per employee. So all this not only causes the manager a lot of lost time and a huge loss of productivity, but also a lot of stress. He becomes alienated from his employees and loses touch with what is really going on in the workplace. And along with that, support for his decisions decreases constantly. All this leaves him with only the illusion of control. Another striking feature of the classic pyramid structure is that there is no room for the most important aspect of the organisation or company, namely 'the customer'. In different sectors, the catch-all term 'customer' is interpreted differently; in a shop it is a potential buyer, in a museum a potential visitor and in a hospital a patient. However, it is very important to realise that 'the customer' or the product should actually be at the centre of every organisation's business structure. After all, without a good product or a satisfied customer, you have no raison d'être or even much likelihood of survival. When we redraw the pyramid from this point of view, we get a completely different picture.

It immediately becomes clear that it is the employees who are closest to the customer or the product and thus play a crucial role in whether or not your organisation succeeds. Therefore, to provide the best service to the customer, you need to have good employees. You'll need to make it easy for them to do their jobs with drive. The manager must be ser-vice-oriented in order to make it possible for employees and teams to do the work going full throttle. In turn, these managers will also need help to take on this role, and so on. In this way, the interconnectedness naturally becomes much greater than in the classic pyramid structure. It is not a rigid subdivision of people 'above' or 'below' each other, but an interplay of subsets all revolving around 'the customer' and the product, which are logically central to everything.

For any organisation, we can say that executive power is determined by how the organisation defines its vision of leadership. What is good leadership for the organisation? What is the desired behaviour the organisation should expect from the executive? When 'the bosses of the bosses' are stuck in a classic hierarchical structure, middle managers may eventually exhibit similar behaviour and be rewarded for it. This in turn, as described above, will influence the behaviour of each individual employee. Traditional hierarchical organisations thus consciously or unconsciously encourage authoritarian leadership, which, as we know by now, is counterproductive. The impact of a paradigm shift to servant-leadership can therefore hardly be overestimated. They have learned this at Semco:

The Brazilian company Semco - formerly a classical, hierarchically structured firm - clearly distanced itself from individual appraisals and the annual evaluation interview. The reasoning was that the position of managers was to facilitate and support the work of employees as best as possible. Therefore, to make the organisation perform better, they introduced bottom-up evaluations of managers, instead of top-down evaluations of employees. Currently, if a manager has two bad evaluations in a row, he is assigned to a different position. Needless to say, managers almost immediately devoted themselves to serving employees' needs. This only benefitted productivity.
(Semler, 2013).

It is very important that an organisation also rewards servant leaders – the ones who let the organisation's interests and purposes take precedence. Fine-tune the expectations in your organisation on this. This is one way to look after yourself, because otherwise, as a leader, you will end up in trouble with your employees, your organisation or both.

To conclude, let me kick in an open door: of course employees are paid by an organisation and in return for this payment, good service should obviously be expected. After all, financial investments like hiring are not done out of charity, but with the aim of achieving results. However, a salary has no impact whatsoever on the satisfaction employees experience with their jobs, as demonstrated by a large-scale, international academic study from 2010 (Judge, 2010). Indeed, the renowned polling company Gallup confirms the previously mentioned results of Rath & Conchie (2008), namely that management style has the greatest influence on results and well-being. To get people to reach their highest performance, you need to take an interest in their motivations, be assertive in judging their performance and strive to instil greater dynamism in them. Now, let us make all this more concrete.

EXERCISE

When is your organisation best satisfied with you as a leader?
Which kind of behaviour does your system reward the most:
authoritarian/directive leadership or servant-leadership?

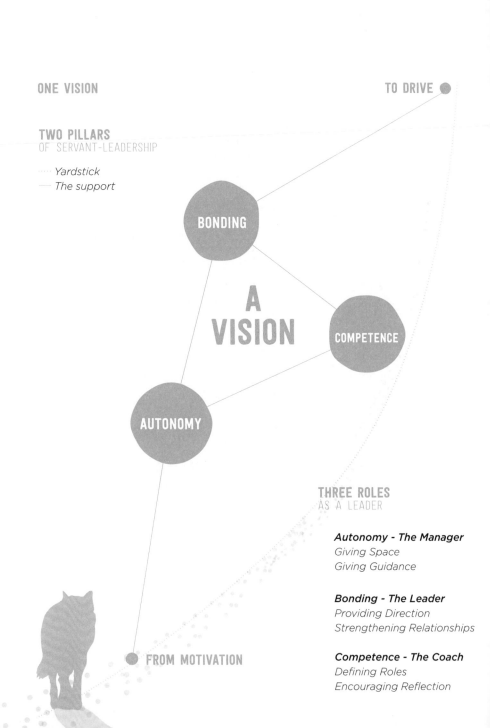

ONE VISION

TO DRIVE

TWO PILLARS
OF SERVANT-LEADERSHIP

····· Yardstick
——— The support

BONDING

A
VISION

COMPETENCE

AUTONOMY

THREE ROLES
AS A LEADER

Autonomy - The Manager
Giving Space
Giving Guidance

Bonding - The Leader
Providing Direction
Strengthening Relationships

FROM MOTIVATION

Competence - The Coach
Defining Roles
Encouraging Reflection

FROM MOTIVATION TO DRIVE

The diagram above summarizes the basis for this book. It will provide a helpful thread throughout the text for clarifying the various facets of servant-leadership. This model makes the connection between the results of the organisation and the needs of the employee. After all, my assumption is that results follow when efforts are made to create drive in the employee. I use the ABC of employee needs mentioned above as a basis for this:

- **Autonomy:** the employee wants to be able to decide for himself, as much as possible, what he does and how he does something.

- **Bonding** with a cause and with the team: the employee wants to contribute to something that is meaningful in his eyes. He wants to do this in connection with the team and the organisation.

- **Competence**: the employee wants to be good at something and be appreciated for his talents.

The servant leader starts with a vision and sets a professional yardstick from there. To achieve it, he will support his employees. He does this from three roles, each linked to the ABC of employee needs:

- **The manager** ensures that the employee is given enough space to perform his job as autonomously as possible. He also facilitates the team's activities by removing as many inefficiencies or obstacles as possible.

- **The leader** ensures that the organisation keeps going in the right direction and that the employee remains relationally connected to the team.

- Finally, there is **the coach**, who ensures proper role allocation based on talents and encourages reflection in a safe learning environment.

These three positions, which I will describe in Part I, provide a basic framework of servant-leadership. In Part II, I will expand on this framework by elaborating on the content of the three roles: we will look at the four styles a manager can apply, the five characteristics that make a servant-leader unique, and the six competences a coach can apply.

The focus of a leader in a team or organisation, in my view, is twofold.

On the one hand, it is about the quality of output: what makes a team achieve results or not? Ultimately, of course, it's results you're aiming for with your team or organisation. In this, I assume that the output (or result) is the direct consequence of the behaviour of the employees. The main question is therefore: how can I ensure that my team exhibits the kind of behaviour that will lead to the best results?

On the other hand, to be tough on results, it is essential to be soft with your employees. After all, to achieve consistently excellent results, it is crucial to give employees what they need to excel. In what follows, I provide theoretical and practical models to help you set the bar high and optimally facilitate the work of your employees.

Above all, remember that many circumstances will always be beyond your control. Think of traffic jams, illness, or international and economic crises. Even on the behaviour of others you can have only indirect influence, but after all, every act of an employee will largely be a reaction to your input and that of the organisation as a whole. Your own behaviour is therefore, in a nutshell, the only thing you can directly influence. One of the basic aspects you can personally influence is that the employee believes in the added value and goals of the organisation. So first, we are going to look at how to instil a strong culture of collective ambition.

PART 1
BASIS

ONE VISION

TO DRIVE

TWO PILLARS

Yardstick
— The support

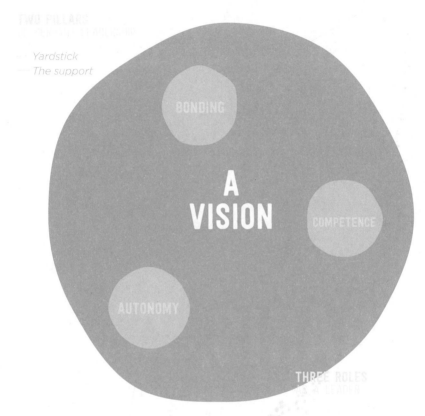

BONDING

A
VISION

COMPETENCE

AUTONOMY

THREE ROLES

Autonomy - The Manager
Giving Space
Giving Guidance

Bonding - The Leader
Providing Direction
Strengthening Relationships

Competence - The Coach
Defining Roles
Encouraging Reflection

ONE VISION

'If you want to build a ship, don't call men together to gather wood, divide the work and give orders. Instead, teach them to long for the vast endless sea.'

— Antoine de Saint-Exupéry

A good ending needs a good beginning. So first of all, as a manager, you need to have a clear understanding of the ultimate goal of your work. What is the 'why' of the work you do as an organisation?

A medieval bishop visits a construction site in the city centre. There he sees three masons, busily at work. He asks the first what he is doing and the latter replies: 'I am scraping the cement off old bricks so we can use them again.' The second replies, 'I am bricklaying a wall.' And the third replies: 'But Monsignor, don't you see ... I am building a cathedral.'

It is absolutely vital that your employee has a proper view of how he or she contributes to a higher purpose. That higher purpose manifests itself in the form of a vision. The vision is what your organisation wants to achieve in its very own way. What it does and how it does it is what sets it apart from other organisations. It is what makes it unique. In my experience, this vision emerges most clearly by answering three key questions:

1. Why are we doing it?
2. What do we stand for?
3. What are we aiming for?

AN ILLUSTRATIVE EXAMPLE:

Joe is a young man who enjoys telling people about his city. He is interested in the history hidden behind the old facades, but at the same time he has an eye for the new graffiti art that has appeared on the wall behind the station. Wanting to share this passion with as many people as possible, he decides to set up a tourism company.

Why is Joe doing it?

He loves guiding and pleasing people with all the facts about his city, so he wants to set up a company to make his passion his profession. Joe believes that the guided tour organised by the city itself is old-fashioned and outdated. He decides that he will set up a young, fresh new tourism company that will showcase his city in a completely different way rather than just through a few dusty churches and the façade of the town hall. It is this vision that will make him an innovator in his city's tourism market.

What does Joe stand for?

What makes Joe unique is his emphasis, which is different from the existing tourism firms in the city. He wants to be young and innovative and propose alternative itineraries that will put his business on the map. He believes the current tourism offering is too limited and that he can tap into the market of younger people who want something 'different' from traditional guides.

What is Joe aiming for?

Joe dreams of employing other young people who are flexible and dynamic in their dealings with customers and who know the cool spots where the outdated, existing tourist itineraries do not go. He wants to invest in targeted advertising so that within two years he will be well-known in the local tourism market with enough turnover in the high season to cover the low season. After three years, he wants to recoup his investment.

Joe formulates challenges for himself. He dreams of what his company could be like in the future. But his vision does not remain in the clouds. He also plans to set concrete financial goals for himself, goals that he hopes his organisation will meet in the (distant) future.

Answering these three questions (Why are we doing it? What do we stand for? What are we aiming for?) provides insight into an organisation's vision. The vision indicates in which direction an organisation hopes to grow. A vision underpins a strategy and can be a reason to say 'no' to ideas or proposals because they threaten to take the organisation or team off course. In this way, a defined vision also sets clear boundaries: we are heading for A, so we will not deviate to point B.

After a year, the city council realised that they were starting to lose many customers to Joe's new company. The councillor in charge of culture approached him to discuss a collaboration. What if their guided city tours could now also be purchased through his organisation?

They had a large client base and Joe would certainly earn a hefty commission from the deal. The councillor was therefore surprised when Joe did not accept his proposal: 'I want to be young and innovative, that's what makes me successful and different,' he had said, 'and I'm not going to just throw that away now, despite the benefits.'

An inspiring vision gets people moving. AMORE is a helpful acronym to use as a checklist, to see whether the vision or goal meets the inspiration test by measuring it against the following criteria:

- Ambitious: does the vision include the essential core of your dream?

- Motivating - Inspiring: do employees see the connection between their own efforts and the vision?

- Original: does the vision interpret the unique DNA of the organisation?

- Relevant: does the vision address all stakeholders, including motivated employees, customers and shareholders?

- Every day: Is the vision formulated in sufficiently concrete terms for it to be tested in every day practice?

EXERCISE

In your organisation, try (together with your team) to answer as concretely as possible the three questions that will unlock the vision. If you find it difficult to come up with concrete answers, try asking yourselves these 'imagination questions' and consider the answers given in the examples.

Why are we doing it?

- imagination questions: What is the raison d'être of our organisation? What is our essence? What would our village/town/world miss if we cease to exist?

- sample response from a residential care centre: We aim to create a homely environment where seniors can spend their old age, a real home where everyone's needs are heard and met, where everyone feels unique and the staff provide space for residents' initiatives.

What do we stand for?

- imagination questions: What are the organisation's core values? In the last six months, there were definitely moments when you and your team shone in performing your tasks. Give an example of these.

- sample answer from a residential care centre: The other day, Jeanine, one of our residents, came to ask if she could lend a hand in preparing the centre's food. She missed cooking at home for her family. Without hesitation, we strapped an apron on her. That afternoon there was soup on the table, prepared entirely according to Jeanine's recipe. Now 'Jeanine's soup' is on the menu every Wednesday.

- leading questions: What underlying values make these moments so powerful? How do you connect them to your vision?

- sample response from a residential care centre: Everyone, from care staff to kitchen staff, has adopted the concept of a customised approach to seniors whenever possible. Our vision includes giving our residents as much personal agency as possible. One way of doing this is by engaging them in tasks they are good at but are no longer able to perform just because they are no longer living independently.

What are we aiming for?

- imagination questions: What do we want to achieve in the future? What is our challenge? What is the organisation's ultimate goal or dream? This dream should be described as clearly as possible and given a fixed time limit. Make it a 'dream with a deadline'.

- sample answer from a residential care home: During their annual team day, the carers work together to draft a fictional newspaper article that could be published within five years. They look back on the unique, humane approach they currently employ. In the newspaper article, they describe how their residential care centre has inspired many other organisations and how, in this way, they have influenced mainstream policy in residential care centres.

A vision only becomes truly interesting if the organisation has made the effort to translate it into the concrete lives of their employees at every possible level. With a clear, supported vision, you can create a shared interest for your employees to rally around. Why are we doing it? What are we working towards as a team? This often creates an extra bond between colleagues because they understand the important goal they are all contributing to. The vision generates meaning and enthusiasm among employees. Recall the ABC of employee needs where B stood for Bonding with a goal and the team. A clear vision empowers employees to commit to something, to become active members of a club they want to belong to.

My experience has taught me that to achieve this, you must not communicate the vision in the abstract - for example, in the company policy statement that employees receive when signing their contract. It is fundamental that you communicate your vision clearly to your employee, so that it is also clear to him within what limits and in which direction he can take initiatives. The servant leader draws attention to the common goal, the shared vision. Even during training and meetings, it is useful to regularly take a moment to discuss it and ask ourselves: are we still on track? Are we as a team - and by extension we as an organisation - still embodying our shared vision?

The basis of all leadership requires a manager able to find people who want to join his vision and who can convince employees to invest in that vision. If this does not happen, and the link between their actions and the vision is not (or no longer) clear to employees, there is a good chance that the desired values and goals will backfire.

Robbie has a passion for all kinds of music, but is particularly on the lookout for the newer trends that rarely reach the general public. He was therefore overjoyed when, after a pleasant chat at a concert, he was offered a job as music programmer for an alternative radio station. The station wanted to play non-commercial music and give a chance to the different subgenres that Robbie appreciated.
In his spare time, Robbie haunted shops in search of new music, constantly contributing new ideas to the station and regularly working overtime to ensure the radio shows were up to scratch. But after a few months, it became clear that management was weighed down by disappointing listening figures. They wanted to change course and play more commercial and accessible music. Robbie initially balked, referring to the station's raison d'être and saying that if they changed the programming now, it would no longer be the job he had signed up for. However, the management persevered.

Robbie settled into his new role, but kept his mouth shut when he had good ideas, only bought music for himself and made sure he was never seen at work before nine o'clock or after six.

The above example reveals the strength of a shared vision and the weakness of a vision that is no longer endorsed by employees. If the vision is shared by the employees who have to do the work, the gain is twofold. The desired behaviour or result is achieved and you create a stimulating, go-ahead environment where employees can consciously seek to align their jobs with their own personal life mission and values. The key question employees ask in this respect is: do I (still) fit in this organisation?

For employees and managers, it is obviously fundamentally important that the answer to this question is yes. A key focus for a manager is to always remain alert to employee initiatives that might enhance the vision. Sometimes these may even be initiatives that challenge the vision at first glance.

Robbie, serving as manager and director of a facility for adults with psychiatric problems, testified:

One day when I was walking down the corridor of the ward, I looked into a room and saw a resident petting a small white dog. It was a beautiful image, but at the same time I knew that our house regulations do not actually allow pets. A conversation with carer Hilde taught me that it was her little dog, and that she had been taking it for a walk around her ward for the past three days after her shift. 'My husband comes to pick me up at work every day. One day he had our Césarke with him.

Some residents who were outside at the time reacted so enthusiastically to the dog that I decided to do a short round through the ward. The reactions of the other residents were so incredibly positive that I was eager to continue taking Césarke around.'

I let Hilde convince me. After all, she pointed out that we wanted as much as possible to be a 'home' for people, considering what their needs might be and stimulating their self-reliance. Moreover, Césarke was greeted with laughter everywhere she went and was well on her way to becoming the department's mascot. I arranged an appointment with Hilde to discuss how we could give Césarke a place with respect for the regulations and for those people who preferred not to have a dog in their room.

In this example, it is clear that Robbie regards his vision, rather than the rules governing it, as the foundation of the organisation. Indeed, Hilde invokes the institution's vision and core values to justify her behaviour, and Robbie immediately understands that this is in line with the direction he and his team want to take. As a manager you can facilitate similar initiatives. Give space to what arises spontaneously. Start from what is there and strengthen that. This is how employees become co-working entrepreneurs.

So, as a very first step towards effective leadership, it is important to dwell on the why of your organisation. From a well-defined vision, it will become clear what can be achieved on a daily basis and how this will happen. These last two questions, the what and the how, take shape within an organisation through a measuring stick and the corresponding support. I discuss these two pillars in the next chapter.

A TOOL FOR YOUR TEAM: METHOD O

When we practice developing a vision, the question we face as a team is both the most essential and the most concise. After all, it challenges us to focus on what exactly makes us different, where our identity lies.

That is why we have cobbled together a handy tool that we use to work with our staff to help forge a vision and create an action plan that everyone supports. Why? Because we have learnt that visions often take off too quickly, fuelled by enthusiasm. But if we are not careful, we miss all the ramifications and dive straight into action, only to realise later that not everyone is on board, or the plans are too vague, or the vision is not sufficiently instilled in our team's DNA.

With Method O, we first make a pit stop to reflect and answer a few questions. And only then do we go full throttle, so that everyone jumps on board at the right time and we get into the right gear together.

We move from 'seeing', through 'connecting', to 'doing'.

It's definitely worth taking a ride with your colleagues through the steps of Method O.

WORKING TOGETHER TOWARDS
A VISION USING METHOD O

SEE

DO

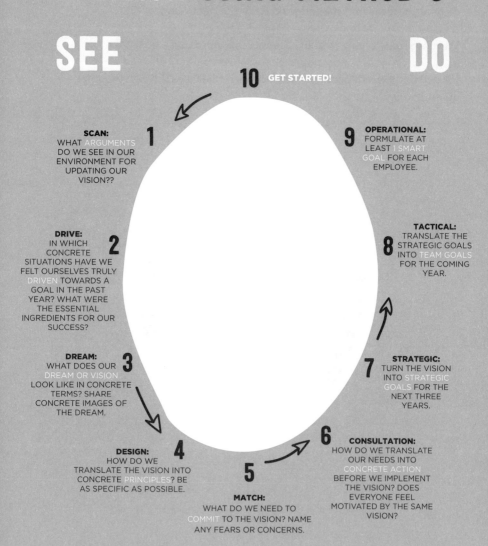

10 GET STARTED!

SCAN:
WHAT ARGUMENTS DO WE SEE IN OUR ENVIRONMENT FOR UPDATING OUR VISION?? **1**

9 **OPERATIONAL:**
FORMULATE AT LEAST 1 SMART GOAL FOR EACH EMPLOYEE.

DRIVE:
IN WHICH CONCRETE SITUATIONS HAVE WE FELT OURSELVES TRULY DRIVEN TOWARDS A GOAL IN THE PAST YEAR? WHAT WERE THE ESSENTIAL INGREDIENTS FOR OUR SUCCESS? **2**

TACTICAL:
TRANSLATE THE STRATEGIC GOALS INTO TEAM GOALS FOR THE COMING YEAR. **8**

DREAM:
WHAT DOES OUR DREAM OR VISION LOOK LIKE IN CONCRETE TERMS? SHARE CONCRETE IMAGES OF THE DREAM. **3**

7 **STRATEGIC:**
TURN THE VISION INTO STRATEGIC GOALS FOR THE NEXT THREE YEARS.

DESIGN:
HOW DO WE TRANSLATE THE VISION INTO CONCRETE PRINCIPLES? BE AS SPECIFIC AS POSSIBLE. **4**

6 **CONSULTATION:**
HOW DO WE TRANSLATE OUR NEEDS INTO CONCRETE ACTION BEFORE WE IMPLEMENT THE VISION? DOES EVERYONE FEEL MOTIVATED BY THE SAME VISION?

5
MATCH:
WHAT DO WE NEED TO COMMIT TO THE VISION? NAME ANY FEARS OR CONCERNS.

CONNECT

RECOMMENDATIONS FOR CREATING THE VISION

- Formulate a strong, defined vision using these three questions:
  Why are we doing it? What do we stand for? What are we aiming for?

- Keep the vision alive among your employees so that they feel
  connected to it and can rally behind it. To zoom in on what you want
  to stand for, take your colleagues through the steps of Method O.
  Make the steps as concrete as possible and return to them repeatedly.

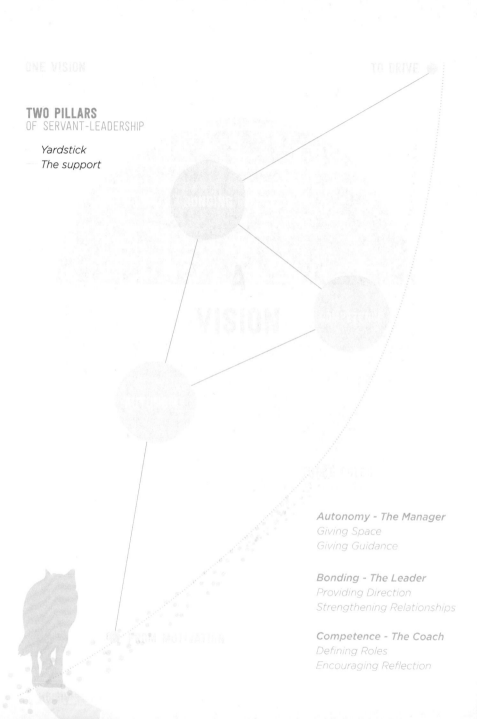

ONE VISION   TO DRIVE

TWO PILLARS
OF SERVANT-LEADERSHIP

Yardstick
The support

Autonomy - The Manager
Giving Space
Giving Guidance

Bonding - The Leader
Providing Direction
Strengthening Relationships

Competence - The Coach
Defining Roles
Encouraging Reflection

TWO PILLARS OF SERVANT-LEADERSHIP

Once your vision is clear to you and your staff, you have to work to achieve it. For this, use two pillars: a yardstick and support. I can explain these concepts most clearly through an example:

> *High jumper Tia Hellebaut may have dreamt of winning the Olympic title early on. She was tall, had a talent for high jumping and her motivation was rock solid. She knew that to make her dream (vision) come true, she had to jump at least 2.05 metres. That was the yardstick. She probably did not get distracted by her friends, who regularly went to parties and told her to enjoy life more. She always went to train when scheduled, driven by her personal ambition and vision. But despite her personal commitment, she soon realised that she needed support. So over time, she enlisted the help of dieticians, athletic trainers and a mental coach. In 2008, she jumped – an unforgettable moment that will go down in Belgian athletics history - over 2.05 metres, becoming the first Belgian high jumper to win Olympic gold.*

These three things - vision, measurement and support - are the framework of any organisation. Tia Hellebaut may not have led a team, but still this example demonstrates what I mean by the two pillars. From your vision, you formulate a yardstick, a concrete goal, a desired outcome. To achieve that result, however, you need support.

As a manager, on the one hand, you monitor your employees' results and the quality of their services, their statistics or their output. On the other hand, you provide the support they need so that they can achieve the standard of performance you expect. Specifically, this involves the integration of management skills (offering direction based on your responsibility as manager) and skills that promote the development of self-organisation (giving space to employees' own responsibility). This is therefore a combined style: a style in which both the effective use of management skills and the effective use of supportive or self-organising skills are developed together in a balanced way. If, in the eyes of employees, these two pillars are not balanced and, for instance, there is too little support for the results a manager asks for, this is experienced as unfair.

In this chapter, I will explain how to formulate a yardstick together with your employees and the importance of dialogue when they fail to measure up to it. Then I will discuss how to shape your support in conversations so they do measure up in the future, or how you can shift the issue in consultations without making concessions regarding the aims of your organisation. By the way, these desired results do not only refer to measurable profitability. They can also refer to the impact of certain actions: attitude, customer loyalty, sales, an improved team atmosphere, etc.

1. THE YARDSTICK

'Vision without action is hallucination.'

— Manfred Kets de Vries, professor of leadership development

Example 1

Consultancy firm DNA puts customer satisfaction first in its vision. They even guarantee that no invoice will be sent if the client is not satisfied with their work. The agreement among the consultants reads: (1) We aim for a customer satisfaction of at least 8.3 out of 10. (2) This should lead to an individual turnover of 105,000 euros on an annual basis.

Example 2

A radio station wants to be a hit station for young people aged 16 to 28 in a socially responsible way. The contract commits a DJ to make a late-night programme that: (1) addresses themes starting with the current living conditions of young people; (2) earns at least 11 percent of market share; (3) offers young people a forum to exchange their experiences.

Example 3

The vision statement of a residential care centre

In our western culture, not so long ago, it was common for several generations to live under the same roof. Today, this is often no longer possible or desirable. For this very reason, we want to focus on creating a homely environment that our seniors enjoy. This is why we constantly ask ourselves two questions: (1) Would I myself want to live here when I am old? (2) Would I let my own family members spend their last phase of life here? As professionals, we want to ensure homeliness by continuing to act with this vision in mind. In this regard, we've made number of social commitments. A selection of commitments on the care centre's meals:

- We prepare tasty food for our seniors.

- We ask our seniors if they have eaten enough
  and if they want anything else.

- We offer meal assistance to our seniors individually,
  not serving two seniors at the same time.

- We don't shout from the food cart.

- We put a bib on our seniors only when it is really necessary.

The above examples show how detailed a yardstick can be, both in terms of behaviour and results. As a manager, it is important that you formulate a clearly understood yardstick for yourself and the organisation. What do you expect from your employees in terms of behaviour and results? What is your standard, the norm that you and your employees must meet?

A yardstick often flows organically from your vision. However, where the vision is about the why, about stating an ideal vision of the future, a yardstick should be about verifiable, concrete daily things. What do you want to see from your employees every day? What results do you want to achieve, and by when?

To make good use of a yardstick and achieve good results, the servant leader goes through five steps:

1. **Functioning of the employee**: the manager checks whether the employee exhibits the desired behaviour within the organisation.

2. **Overview**: the manager routinely follows up on agreements and responsibilities.

3. **Results**: the manager checks whether the desired results are being achieved, if possible using Critical Performance Indicators (CPIs). These are fixed indicators that determine when it is possible to claim success.

4. **Time monitoring**: the manager checks whether the results are achieved within the predetermined time frame.

5. **Evaluating**: the manager evaluates the previous four steps and, together with the employee, looks at what can be improved and how to achieve it.

The five initial letters form the acronym FORTE (Italian for 'strong'). This is a reminder to keep your actions constantly oriented towards results.

EXERCISE

- Considering the examples above, formulate a yardstick for your organisation: What behaviour do you wish to see? What results should be achieved? Avoid vague descriptions and state as concretely as possible what is expected.

- Check with your employees: Do they understand the yardstick you will be using? Does the team know what behaviour and concrete results are expected?

All employee behaviour should be capable of assessment: Is it acceptable or unacceptable to me? Is it below or above the yardstick? In general, consider the yardstick as an imaginary line. Above the line is acceptable behaviour and below the line is unacceptable behaviour. Servant-leadership is about being a manager who creates the right conditions for employees to function optimally.

Servant-leadership has nothing to do with walking around and checking whether people are at their desks. The servant leader makes a switch from 'I control' to 'I trust'. He does not do this blindly, but by leading employees towards greater autonomy and team bonding. Ideally, the manager and the employee agree on a clear framework that allows for autonomy and flexibility. Naturally, it is key not to let this autonomy turn into anarchy. It is important that the manager and the employee keep the lines of communication wide open vis-à-vis each other and the team.

Charlotte heads the administrative department of a company that supports organisations with IT solutions. Her co-worker Hannah sits with her at a work station. Hannah provides customers with telephone support for operational problems. She does her job extremely well: she is very helpful and customer-friendly. She even once put up a poster in the office saying: 'You only have one chance to make a good first impression.' Charlotte notices for the first time that in spite of all her drive, Hannah sometimes answers the phone with: 'Yes, this is Hannah' even when speaking to outside lines. Hannah herself is socially adept enough to resolve this charmingly. Precisely because she can always add a quip to the conversation, she does not realise that her manner may come across as strange to a customer.

For Charlotte, Hannah's behaviour is below professional standards. It seems clear that Charlotte must encourage Hannah to change her ways. Yet Charlotte fails to raise the issue with Hannah. In my experience, managers have thoughts throughout the day that they never voice. Many of these thoughts are about their employees' behaviour and how this behaviour measures on the yardstick. Sometimes managers 'forget' to praise their employees when they achieve their results and do the right thing (the huge importance and power of appreciation is discussed in Chapter 6). However, it is also common for managers to notice that their employees' behaviour doesn't measure up, but still decide to keep it to themselves. This happens out of not wanting to demoralize employees, to remain a well-liked manager, not letting on that you might be dissatisfied... However, waiting too long to raise issues can create even bigger problems in the long run:

- The manager is not taking good enough care of himself. Soon, the unacceptable behaviour becomes his problem: after all, it bothers him.
- If he says nothing, it eats up his energy.

- It can affect his perceptions of the employee (from: 'He sometimes forgets', to: 'Oh, he's just nonchalant').

- As frustrations pile up, the manager may no longer manage to say things in a relaxed manner, even when there is actually not much going on.

- If the manager isn't careful, employees may perceive this as inconsistent and therefore questionable.

- The longer the manager waits to call out unacceptable behaviour, the harder it eventually becomes and the less the employees will accept it, precisely because of all the eye-rolling that had gone on before.

So, when you notice behaviour that falls below your professional standards, it is very important to provide the necessary support to ensure change. This 'support' often takes other forms in some companies. For instance, financial bonuses may be promised to employees who meet certain quotas. However, several studies refute the effectiveness of such means (Judge et al., 2010). Motivating an employee with extrinsic rewards does not lead to better results in the long run and may even lead to the employee becoming less of a team player. Because he is rewarded, he is tempted to work towards his own personal gain, not the team's gain. Moreover, bonuses do not always paint a fair picture. Excellent effort is not always rewarded.

The reverse is also true: sometimes individuals benefit dispropor-tionately from the team's performance or other factors, if one were only considering their own effort and contribution. Therefore, such individual reward mechanisms are not really a viable system in the long run if you want to encourage people to perform above the yardstick. A more sustainable method is to evoke and sharpen intrinsic motivation. You do this by engaging in dialogue with your employee, listening and looking for improvement together. Support is all about dialogue.

2. SUPPORT

'You cannot grow businesses.
You can only grow people that grow businesses.'

— Tex Gunning, CEO TNT Express

So the two pillars of servant-leadership are making expectations explicit and providing support for the employee's performance. If your yardstick is clearly understood, you naturally want your employee to respect it. However, how can you communicate your expectations to an employee without making him feel that those expectations are being forced on him? How do you approach this in such a way that the employee experiences it as supportive? How do you guarantee sufficient support and commitment from the employee?

Lois works as a head nurse in the terminal ward of a large hospital. On Mondays, sometimes her PC is covered with Post-it reminders, accounts of things that did or didn't happen over the weekend, and so on. Nurse Sheila did the weekend shift. He noted that their patient Jules had suddenly deteriorated sharply. It is the organisation's view that family members should then be informed at once. A member of the care team is expected to notify the family or partner immediately in such cases. Yet this did not happen. Taking the organisation's vision as a starting point, Lois feels this is not okay.

Suppose she ultimately chooses not to discuss it with Sheila. She does not take the time to do so and instead conducts the 'bad news' conversation with Jules's partner herself.

EXERCISE

- What are the consequences for Lois? For Sheila?
  For the team members? For their relationship?

- Think about your team members' performances over the past week. Which behaviour was acceptable? Which behaviour was not entirely OK?

To make a strong team, members must feel free to have conversations about each other's responsibilities. From whatever position you conduct these supportive conversations, they always follow the same four steps. When you notice that a certain behaviour is below par, address your employee. First let the employee say their piece, then discuss the matter together and finally agree on a solution (Karssing, 2006). By doing so, you create a comfortable atmosphere for addressing issues should another problem arise. So, following on from the above example, Lois decided to address Sheila.

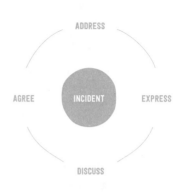

1. Express

Let your employees express their needs and expectations regarding the workplace. Be genuinely curious about this. If you are too quick to counter with the organisation's expectations, you will meet with resistance. It is important that the employee be given the chance to tell their side of the story.

> Lois tells Sheila she is curious to know where he came up with the initiative to write the post-it. Sheila indicates that he does realise that the patient's partner would receive the information later than is desirable from the organisation's point of view.

2. Discuss

Discuss with your team members each other's interests, views, needs and dilemmas. Also clearly state your expectations of the employee. It is important to set clear lines, explain the vision of the organisation and emphasise certain choices. Be aware that experiences on the shop floor may require different procedures from those initially proposed by managers. Through your exchange, you create a solid psychological basis for dealing with one another.

Sheila admits he finds it difficult to have a 'bad-news' conversation. He does not know exactly how to start it. He feels very insecure and is afraid that family members would sense this and no longer trust him. To be able to do this in the future, he needs support.

3. Agree

Once both parties have expressed their concerns and discussed them thoroughly, you move on to agreements on how to actually act. You can record these agreements as procedures or objectives. I often observe that no clear agreements were made between managers and their employees, which they could later use to call each other to account. The agreements were too non-committal or not sufficiently concrete, making it difficult and sometimes even impossible to confront each other. For concrete results, make sure your agreements or objectives are SMART (Reddin, 1989):

- **S**pecific. Is the agreement unambiguous?

- **M**easurable. Can we verify and measure that the agreement has been carried out?

- **A**cceptable. Is the agreement acceptable to employees, customers and/or management?

- **R**ealistic. Is the agreement achievable?

- **T**ime-bound. When do we get feedback on the agreement? When should the objective be achieved and evaluated?

An aspiration can be vague or visionary, but targets are more concrete and put people to work. If an agreement is SMART, you can safely and clearly expect results.

In a brief chat, Lois and Sheila come to an agreement. They agree that Sheila will conduct at least two (measurable) 'bad-news' conversations in the next month (time-bound) with patients' family members (specific). This will be under Lois's guidance, so that Sheila feels supported and can follow Lois's recommendations (acceptable). They both consider this feasible (realistic).

4. Address

Only when the above cycle has been completed can you really begin to hold each other to an agreement. Many agreements are made on the basis of performance, coaching or assessment interviews. But sometimes it also helps to make less explicit rules of conduct discussable in the corridors.

Ellen and Sofie work in the council's maintenance department. Team leader Jordan listens in on a conversation they have about a close colleague. 'That Karen, we can't do anything with her. Every day she forgets something, and she's always interrupting our cleaning round. She doesn't like being here. It's as if she only does it for the money.

For Jordan, such statements are actually not OK, and don't measure up on his yardstick. He addresses them about the issue. Jordan lets them talk quietly, is curious about their story and asks how they are dealing with the situation (speaking out).

He discusses what the effects might be if they do not support their colleague, or point out to her at the moment when it happens how her repeatedly forgetting material affects them. He says he understands that this is not helpful, but adds that Karen can't do much about it if you don't tell her that it bothers you or if you can't offer tips on how to remember everything she needs to bring (discuss).

Together they agree that Ellen will calmly address Karen about this herself. Jordan asks for feedback on this tomorrow to hear how the conversation went (agreeing and addressing).

A BALANCE BETWEEN MEASURING AND SUPPORT

The yardstick sharpens your expectations. It concretely defines what you want to see from your employees every day. However, common sense preaches that the higher these expectations, the more support your employees need. As a manager, there is no point in passing judgement on someone's failing to measure up, if you are not curious about what went wrong or are unwilling to offer more support, enabling your employee to do better next time.

The support of a servant leader is obviously not limited to the four steps discussed. The above example only outlines the general course of a supportive conversation. It will only become concrete when used from one of the three positions you assume as a servant-leader: manager, leader or coach. I discuss these positions in more detail in the next section.

A TOOL FOR YOUR TEAM

We developed a tool for creating a yardstick together with your team.
The team portfolio allows you to clarify team goals, team agreements,
individual roles and individual initiatives.

EXERCISE

Complete the team portfolio together with your colleagues' and
experience the motivation that a clear yardstick can bring to your team.

MY PORTFOLIO

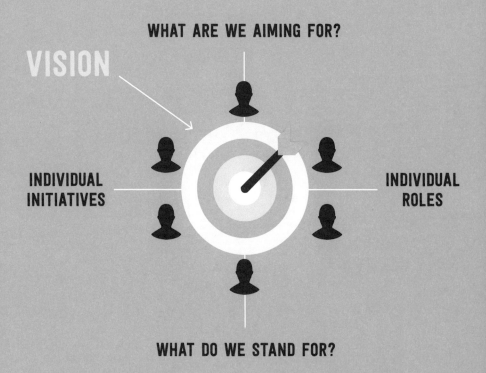

WHAT ARE WE AIMING FOR?

VISION

INDIVIDUAL INITIATIVES

INDIVIDUAL ROLES

WHAT DO WE STAND FOR?

WHAT ARE WE AIMING FOR TOGETHER?

Our ambition for the coming year:

Our focus areas:

Some smart goals:

Questions to get you started

What is our collective ambition? Where do we want to be in the coming year? Which domains do we as a team want to focus on in the coming year? How do we translate this into a SMART objective for the next 3 months? Which objectives are relevant to me? Who follows up on the objectives? How do we measure progress? When will we be satisfied? How will we celebrate our successes?

WHAT DO WE STAND FOR TOGETHER?

Agreements & rules around consultation, decisions, procedures...

Living rules, how to give and receive feedback, how to deal with conflicts:

Questions to get you started

What kind of (team) consultation do we need? Which decisions can be taken individually? Which ones as a team? What rules or procedures apply to everyone and across all teams? What tools or instruments are there that can help us do our work, or develop competences, skills and knowledge?

What are the precepts - in line with our values - that we adhere to? Do we know each other well enough to use each other's strengths and to understand each other? How do we give each other feedback? How can we use conflict to our advantage?

INDIVIDUAL & TEAM ROLES

My core role

My expertise role

My team role

INDIVIDUAL INITIATIVES

Day in, day out we go full steam ahead to fulfil our collective ambition. At the same time, we also want to care about you as an individual. That is why we occasionally hold conversations.

The following questions can help shape these conversations.

	Tell me...	What concrete initiative I can take away from this conversation??
What was/were your top moment(s) last year?		
What is a concrete ambition of yours?		
What would you like to change in the way we work? What can you do about it?		
What concrete ideas do you have to improve bonding within the team?		
In which areas do you think you can still grow?		
Do you have any tips to help your manager grow?		

RECOMMENDATIONS ON THE YARDSTICK AND THE SUPPORT

- Set a clear yardstick.

- Discuss with your team whether the yardstick (desired result, desired behaviour) is clear. Be sure to praise achieved results or desired behaviour.

- When you notice people underperforming, don't hesitate to call them on it.

- Let your employees speak their piece, then discuss the problem. This will also allow you to address them

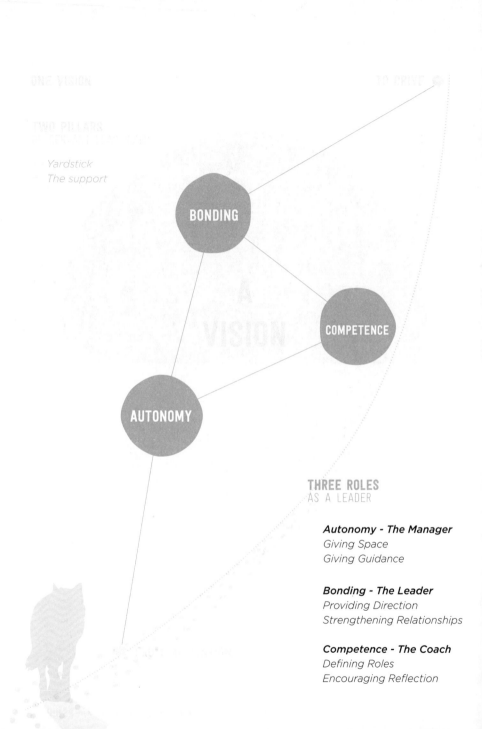

ONE VISION TO DRIVE

TWO PILLARS

Yardstick
The support

BONDING

A
VISION

COMPETENCE

AUTONOMY

THREE ROLES
AS A LEADER

Autonomy - The Manager
Giving Space
Giving Guidance

Bonding - The Leader
Providing Direction
Strengthening Relationships

Competence - The Coach
Defining Roles
Encouraging Reflection

THREE ROLES AS A SERVANT-LEADER

Earlier in this book we saw how a servant leader formulates a yardstick for his employees from his vision and provides the necessary support so that the yardstick is realised. In this chapter, I discuss the three alternating roles of the manager.

Because servant-leadership connects the needs of the organisation and the employee, it makes sense that these three roles are linked to the aforementioned ABC of employee needs: **autonomy, bonding** with the organisation and **competence**. Linked to these are the three roles of manager, leader and coach.

The **manager** steers for results. His thoughts are results-oriented; he knows well what individual contributions to expect from employees and sets clear criteria to meet the desired outcome. With this approach, he gives space to employees and encourages autonomy. He also coordinates activities, resources and responsibilities effectively and efficiently.

The **leader** is responsible for ensuring that his team moves in the right direction. He makes sure that there is no deviation from professional standards. He also monitors the relationship between himself and his team on one hand and between team members on the other.

Only when the roles of manager and leader are properly filled will there be an opportunity for the servant leader to do full justice to his role as **coach**. He ensures that everyone ends up at the right task and that employees are motivated to use their talents as much as possible.

In this way, he strives to customise the development of competences in each employee. He also ensures a safe learning climate through reflection, creating a learning and feedback culture within the team.

INTRODUCTORY EXERCISE ON THE THREE ROLES

Think for a moment about how you divide your time as a manager between the three positions of manager, leader and coach. Draw the following pie charts:

- as your current role looks to you today;

- the way your employees expect you to perform your job;

- the way your own supervisor/ director expects you to perform your job;

- as you think it should look from your current role, exactly as you would like it.

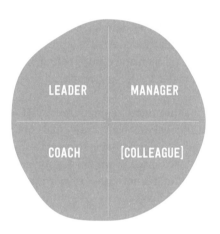

Additional questions (group work):

- Is there room on your current pie chart for the three tasks of a leader (manager-leader-coach)? If not, what is missing?

- What expectations do employees and the management set for you? Do the two match each other? How do you personally deal with this?

- In what ways does your current pie chart differ from your ideal pie chart? What can you do about this?

-

1. THE MANAGER: FOCUS ON AUTONOMY

'Let whoever sweeps the floor choose their own broom.'

— Howard Behar

To begin, let us return for a moment to the example of the wolf pack. Indeed, when we think about an executive in his role as a manager, there are some striking similarities.

Leadership in wolves, as described above, is not based on a hierarchical, authoritarian way of doing things, but on an outgrowth of complex social contacts. The alpha male regularly makes decisions that illustrate this. For example, he will 'lead' the hunt, but during the hunt, each member of the pack has the freedom (and thus responsibility) to make their own choices. Only by allowing this space to each member does the pack manage to function effectively as a group and achieve its goals.

The effectiveness of wolves is determined by a vital pattern of tasks in which each wolf plays its part. The pack streamlines the pattern to fit a whole range of external variables: weather, environment, light, likelihood of outcome and necessity. But internal factors also come into play: the relationships between pack members, the mating season and the division of roles. For example, when a particular wolf has more experience in a sector of their territory, it will be this wolf, regardless of its 'status', who leads the pack because it has a better idea of where they might find food. When a female wolf goes hunting, other wolves will stay behind to look after the pups. The pack is able to adapt efficiently to changing circumstances through its flexibility. Each member strives to improve its abilities, based on previous experiences, to get the best possible result.

Making each member of the team the owner of the solution and maintaining a strong organisational structure are two features you need to bring to fruition in your role as manager.

In the role of manager, the executive is in charge of:
- Making sure that his team has the **necessary space** to achieve the planned results. In mutual consultation, he ensures clear objectives, procedures, agreements and good planning, allowing the employee to work as autonomously as possible.

- **Guiding** his team. He tries to create a structure in which his employees can work optimally by co-ordinating activities, resources and responsibilities effectively and efficiently.

GIVING SPACE THROUGH STEERING FOR OUTPUT

A caricature of the classic image of a manager is someone constantly giving specific orders: you do this now, you do that now. As a manager, you and your team aim for great results. Some directives (e.g. on behaviour) are best given concretely and directly. In Part 2, we will see how this style can be effective when it is advantageous to be perfectly clear on expectations or where instruction makes sense.

A servant leader strives to allow his employees as much autonomy and responsibility as possible. The word responsibility sums it up nicely: making employees more responsible is essentially about increasing their ability to respond to different situations (Clement, 2008). He will always try to give them as much space and decision-making power as possible. One way to put this into practice is by steering them by criteria rather than solutions. This is called output steering.

Output steering means that professionals are given enough space to work within their own field to find solutions to goals. After all, it is operational employees who can achieve (operational) excellence (Vandendriessche & Clement, 2006). The desired result is achieved on the basis of set criteria, so the employee feels ownership of the project and can arrange the work according to his own rhythm and insight, without having to worry about the desired result, as you can see in this example:

> *Your team's coffee machine is broken and cannot be repaired. Manager Erik asks Sofie from administration to buy a coffee machine. He tells her to ask the team what kind they would like.*
> **Erik**: *"We have a budget of 200 euros.*
> **Erika**: *'I think it's important that it has a two-litre water tank.'*
> **Tom and Yasid**: *'We want fresh coffee. The machine should be able to grind coffee.'*
> **Laura**: *'It has to be able to hold at least two big cups at a time.'*
> **Erik**: *"The organisation demands at least a two-year warranty when buying new appliances.*
> **Michael**: *'The machine has to be black, because that suits our meeting room best.'*

We can think of correctly-set criteria as an enclosed space in which to work. Imagine the space as a meadow. The criteria set by the manager are the posts around which the fence is stretched, as wide apart as possible. They provide a comfortable and clear framework within which each employee can express his creativity, expertise or operational excellence. In this way, the manager uses criteria to limit the possibilities within which employees may act. The result or 'solution' will automatically be located within the confines of this meadow; it is defined by this meadow, as it were. If the end result does not meet the criteria, it's a failure. So the solution flows from the direction defined by the criteria,

although several solutions or ways of approach are still possible. Here, Erik could have simply told Sofie to go buy a coffee machine that was on sale. He doesn't, however. He gives her the criteria that the machine must meet and then lets her look for solutions herself. This gives Sofie responsibility and a say in choosing the coffee machine. Of course, replacing a coffee machine is not a very complex problem.
In the workplace, bigger challenges present themselves.

At the editorial office of The Times, managing editor Steven wants an article on the events regarding Heritage Open Days. He convenes an editorial board meeting to listen to their ideas; the deadline is looming, as it is every day.

According to the general model, we can say that the professional yardstick is the very first criterion to be met. From there, the manager can set out other criteria or 'fence posts' to create an 'empty' space in which employees can move around. As a manager, use your professionalism and expertise from experience to help think about criteria.

Often, there will be 'hard' criteria fixed in advance (e.g. the professional yardstick, budget and time allotted, fixed by the organisation), although there are usually other criteria that can be formulated by mutual agreement. After all, it is important to create the right working space for the professional.
By having a constructive dialogue about criteria, the employees' feeling of ownership is increased. Moreover, this makes it everyone's responsibility to make sure no criteria are accidentally overlooked.

Because using this method creates space and clarity, it gives both managers and employees a mighty boost to their energy and self-management. Being able to steer by criteria instead of by solutions reduces stress for the managers and builds trust, space, motivation and responsibility for executive employees.

As managers have more knowledge and experience of operational procedures, there may be a temptation for them to devise or implement solutions themselves. However, this is the employees' domain. To fully empower your employees, it is better to leave the operational execution (and successes) to them as much as possible.

During the editorial board, the young journalist Iris mentions that there is a historic castle on the hill a little further away. They have organised medieval festivals there and it seems like an interesting topic. However, Steven orders her to gather some information regarding the ancient abbey in the area. When Iris returns, he takes her notes and quickly writes an article on the renovation of the mill near the abbey. Iris is irritated that she does not get the chance to write an interesting piece about it herself.

Looking at this example, it is clear that results can suffer if employees are not managed according to their ABC requirements. This is where the need for autonomy and competence comes into play. Steven does not give his employee the opportunity to work on her own, which reduces her autonomy. Steven's decision may (for example) have been driven by the fear that Iris's piece would not meet the newspaper's standards, which would mean that he would have to work on it afterwards anyway. However, Steven could have avoided this scenario by setting clear criteria. For example, he could have specified everything that was important to him (for example: the text must be well written with a 500-550 word count, the monument must be known in the area, the deadline must be respected and it must be accompanied by a good photo). Using his criteria, we would get something like this:

From the example on the right, we can clearly see that the solution can only exist if all the criteria are met. The solution remains 'the same' (a good article for a regional newspaper supplement), but in this case Iris is responsible for creating an appropriate solution herself. Steven too has nothing to fear when he sends out his young journalist. Indeed, if any of the criteria are not met, he is in a position to challenge Iris about it.

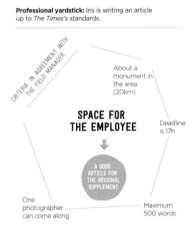

Professional yardstick: Iris is writing an article up to *The Times's* standards.

About a monument in the area (20km)

SPACE FOR THE EMPLOYEE

Deadline is 17h

CRITERIA IN AGREEMENT WITH THE FIELD MANAGER

A GOOD ARTICLE FOR THE REGIONAL SUPPLEMENT

One photographer can come along

Maximum 500 words

If we steer by output, we as managers will only have to set the criteria to determine a solution. This allows the employee to decide how to complete the task. The trick is to avoid forcing a solution and to steer towards achieving the agreed criteria (output). Otherwise, there will be no autonomy and employees may feel patronised, which can lead to tensions. So a manager can really afford to have no solutions ('Oy, it's Heritage Open Days; what will this article be about?'). He just can't afford not to have criteria, because without criteria, after all, employees lose their framework (for an interesting elaboration of this theme, see Vandendriessche & Clement, 2006).

Again, the servant leader should always be engaging in dialogue with his employees. For instance, an employee who has only just started working may need specific rules of action to come up with a proper solution (think, a smaller 'meadow'). However, if you keep doing this as the employee's competence improves, it will come across as patronising. On the other hand, if you leave too much space to your employee (bigger 'meadow'), there will be ambiguity about what exactly is expected. Employees who are still learning on the job will need to be guided in this. How to adapt your style as a manager to the capabilities of the employee, and even to the capabilities of your team, I explain in Chapter Four.

So, to sum up: if you are satisfied with their work, competent and motivated professionals will tell you the criteria they need to operate. You don't need to fill in how they take that further. During a feedback day, a manager once told me: 'I make sure there is some kind of highway and that highway leads one way. But it's my people who decide which car they go in, how fast they go, whether they fill up, whether they take a turn, whether there are three of them in the car, and so on. It's up to them to see where we end up.' Restated: give your employees leeway so they can work as professionals.

EXERCISE

Think of a task you want to give to an employee. Try to stay at the criteria level only.

GUIDING THE FLOW OF TASKS

About 60 per cent of employee complaints in organisations are related to three factors not being optimally co-ordinated:

1. **What** is the sequence of tasks? Are they in a logical sequence?
2. **Who** is responsible for which job? And with what remit?
3. **How** is a task supported? For example, are there (technological) tools available?

An important responsibility of the manager is to make sure that the interaction between these three factors happens as smoothly as possible. Each team has one or more task streams it is responsible for. There is often a logical sequence of jobs to perform, step by step. In the process, something changes with each step and a goal is ultimately realised.

For a builder's team in the construction industry, this could go as follows:

Receipt of the new order → preparation of a work schedule → discussion of the work schedule at team level → installation on site → progressive implementation of the work according to the schedule → dismantling and clearing the site → final inspection and/or handover → evaluation → invoicing.

A manager (together with his staff) should have a clear view of the jobs taking place in and around his team and how they interact. To do this, it helps to create a map combining all the tasks. A job plan visualises what the successive tasks are (what), the associate responsible (who) and resources (how). In this way, it becomes a useful tool when discussing tasks with people outside the team or the team members themselves.

In een ziekenhuis op de afdeling Inwendige Geneeskunde zou dat de volgende activiteitenstroom kunnen zijn:

administrative admission of patient → physical admission, welcoming and installation → preparation of a care plan → communication of the care plan to all involved → cyclical and/or progressive implementation of the care plan → physical discharge and farewell → administrative discharge → billing.

Where do we (often) need to redo things? Where do employees need support the most? Where do I often get called upon as manager? Where am I usually putting out fires? Can we reduce certain recurring customer complaints about one or more tasks?

On top of that, it is important to know who takes on which jobs and what tools are provided to them. By tools, we mean things that support the team's activities and ensure that the job plan is optimal (predictable, error-free, fast, etc.). This is often done by automating the flow of information or standardising ways of working. This can be done through checklists, standard forms, procedures, rules, templates, calculation methods, software, communication systems, IT systems, work instructions, and so on.

Finally, it is essential that the right person is in the right place. Is it always clear who is in charge of implementing the task? Who is involved in which step and with what mandate? Does this work for everyone?

EXERCISE

List your team's main tasks in a logical order. Is the order really logical? Does a loss of efficiency crop up anywhere? Are employees supported with the right tools at all times? Is the right man or woman in the right place? With the right mandate?

Do this exercise together with your employees.

Activity	Responsible person	Tools

Such a job plan is best made with your team. By compiling it together, a lot of pain points and suggestions usually emerge spontaneously. A good way to resolve certain pain points is the improvement board.

The improvement board consists of five steps. The first superficially describes the problem, the second looks for any underlying or essential problem, and the third describes a basis to use towards a sensible goal to fix it. Then we work upwards again. By taking into account certain established criteria (step 4), you can arrive at possible solutions in the fourth and fifth steps.

Situation: Problem/Cause

Write down the problem

E.g. We have too little
office space –
this is frustrating.

**What solutions do we have?
What is possible?**

E.g. Looking together at what are
necessary agenda items (does
everything have to be decided in
the group?)
E.g. Forwarding the meeting
agenda so that everyone can
prepare (saving time)

**Why is the problem
occurring?**

Analyse the problem: why is it a
problem? What is the cause of the
problem? What can we influence?
Formulate the essential problem

Bijv. We meet too often and for too
long and with too many people

**Check if there are criteria before
you brainstorm solutions. What is
already certain? Is there a
framework within which to think?**

E.g. We only have one meeting
room
E.g. We need to meet at least once
a month

Define a sensible goal

Make sure it is about results or
commitments and not statements
of intentions

E.g. We want to have fewer
meetings (want = intend)
E.g. We are going to ensure a
significant decrease in the number
of meetings so that we have
enough space

WHO DOES
WHAT WHEN?

By using an improvement board, you have a visual and transparent way to consult efficiently and work together on shared goals. For instance, teams may learn that they don't have to involve everyone in a briefing, that they don't have to write an extensive report but that a to-do list is sufficient, that you can save a lot of time with a few small tweaks. It is an effective way to expose bureaucratic tensions. On top of that, making a schedule is less intimidating to teams because here tasks are disconnected from people and linked to the function. That way, it is easier to talk about flaws because guilt is less of an issue. Once you are able to put your finger on a wound, you can heal it by looking for cures with the team. That way, in the long run, every experience, complaint, problem or frustration can become an opportunity to optimise the work process.

However, some challenges come not from within the company, but from outside. It is important when analysing the flow of tasks to also identify factors that cannot be controlled - for instance, if you are dependent on external sources. Sometimes there are jobs that rely on people or organisations outside the team. Many managers tend to intervene when a problem arises between an outside organisation and their own team.

Tim is business manager of three different restaurants. He has good contacts with a vegetable supplier who comes to deliver every Tuesday morning. Recently, however, deliveries have been delayed several times, with dire consequences.

Of course Tim can take on the responsibility himself of contacting the supplier and holding him accountable for delays. However, this leads Tim to commit to having such conversations in the future with every external supplier he depends on (the butcher, the window cleaner, the wine merchant, and so on). The unintended or unwanted effect of this is that the team becomes dependent on the manager. After all, he is the one who puts out the fires; he's the problem-solver. From the philosophy of servant-leadership, we want to systematically make the team as independent as possible from the leader.

So the leader will have to ask himself: do I dare to let go of some of my tasks, my authority? Can I deal with the idea that by redefining my role, I may be redefining my job?

Tim decides it's best to leave that kind of communication to the cooking teams in his restaurants. He calls them and tells them to contact the vegetable supplier to bring up the problem of delays. That way, on one hand, they can be quicker on the ball if it happens again and, on the other hand, the staff will have mastered this task if Tim is ever unavailable. He also makes it clear that the cooking teams should keep him informed if another delay occurs.

EXERCISE

Look at your job plan:

* Where do people struggle to carry out the tasks expected of them? Are they dependent on external services in those places?

* .Where can you optimise connections with outside services so that your people are not always dependent on you?

* Is the relationship with the external services as good as it could be?

* Is their own team's work sometimes hindered by other teams' failure to deliver results on time?t

* Is it advantageous for you as manager to facilitate your team's work by engaging with outside services yourself or is your team ready to take on this responsibility?

RECOMMENDATIONS FOR THE SERVANT-MANAGER

- Try to stay as far away from 'solutions' as possible.
  Train yourself to give your employees criteria to work with.
  Allow your employees to excel at what they are good at.

- Check regularly with your employees to see whether
  you are giving them too many criteria (patronising)
  or too few (unclear). Enter into dialogue.

- Establish a job plan and, together with your team, try to streamline
  it as effectively as possible using the improvement board.

2. THE LEADER: FOCUS ON BONDING

If you change the way you look at things,
the things you look at change.

— *Wayne Dyer*

The alpha wolf leads the way most of the time, determining the direction of the pack. He forges a path through deep snow to conserve the energy of pack members following in his wake. When leading younger wolves on less rugged terrain, he walks behind them and directs them with discreet signals. He is able to relinquish his leadership role, while always determining the overall direction of the pack.

Apart from glances, wolves use numerous ways to communicate, including body language, subtle caresses, playful snapping, running away and, of course, the most familiar of all: howling. There is still no conclusive explanation as to why wolves howl and what they are telling each other by doing so, but today's assumptions are drastically different from the clichéd view that howling was related to loneliness or aggression. Employing as many as 21 different tones in their howls, wolves respond to impending danger, mourning, friendship, greetings, searching for pack members and, in all likelihood, simply pleasure. Wolves in a pack never howl in the same way, but always make sure that each produces a different sound so that they sound stronger as a group. The famous general Ulysses S. Grant wrote in his diary that on a visit to Texas he heard the howls of as many as "thirty to forty" wolves at night. When they finally caught sight of the animals, they turned out to be only two.

So determining direction is important as a leader, but so is communication. Some biologists argue that howling is a phenomenon of fundamental importance for the relationships between wolves and that a pack will fall apart without howling. This is just as true for humans: communication is critical to relationships within an organisation.

In the role of leader, the executive safeguards:

- That there is no deviation from the chosen direction (the vision and the yardstick).
- That relationships are relaxed and efficient between himself and the team and within the team.

LEADING THE WAY AND MONITORING THE VISION

A crucial role of the manager is that of leader. The leader ensures everyone is acting from an ambitious, shared and supported vision. He is able to ignite enthusiasm for the way forward, using his vision to reach certain objectives and metrics). He can coordinate an employee's personal objectives with those of the organisation. How to achieve this was covered in Chapter 1.

But a servant leader also has a vision for collaboration. Usually, teams have firm opinions about what they see as desirable outcomes, customer focus or good service. They know within each assignment, vision and mission statement where they allowed to collaborate and can relate to it. But whether or not you achieve these objectives largely depends on the quality of the relationships within your team. So developing your own vision for cooperation and communication with your team is crucial. The following section provides a starting point.

STRENGTHENING RELATIONSHIPS BY USING CIRCULAR VISION

Many executives often experience the same challenges when it comes to communication and collaboration: how do you deal with information about colleagues that comes via third parties? What do you do about unspoken conflicts? Are there past wounds that still have an impact today? What can you do when you address people about their behaviour and their behaviour doesn't change?

Linear and circular vision
We have been trained or brought up to think and look at behaviour in terms of cause and effect. Because another person is extremely rude to me, I freak out. Because the other person is so stubborn, progress is blocked. Here, we mainly look at who did what to whom. We call this linear viewing. My behaviour is a 'reaction' to the other person's behaviour. It is perfectly 'logical' that we view personal relationships through these glasses. In my view, it's actually a matter of perspective: we see what happens in front of our eyes, but less easily register what we ourselves are doing and how that affects the other person. After all, the other person's behaviour cannot be disconnected from my own.

For a moment consider the people around you. The image each person has of you is different, right? Some are more likely to perceive you as thoughtful, while others more likely to think you are funny. It makes sense, because each person triggers a slightly different version of you every time you interact. This game of mutual influencing goes on and on. Everything you do is not only a response to another's behaviour, it also triggers new behaviour as a reaction. The latter forms the essence of circular vision. I do things that the other person interprets in a certain way; he then reacts, eliciting new interpretations and behaviour from me, with which I elicit a new round of interpretations and behaviour from him, and so on. Hence our behaviour goes around in a circle and not as one-way traffic.

Seeing through linear and circular glasses offers different ways of looking at our behaviour. Linear viewing may well suffice for technical content. But people are more complex. And that's when linear viewing falls short. Either I recognise that my behaviour is related to the other person's behaviour and I therefore have a stake in it, or I do not. I have to recognise that there is a pattern in our interactive behaviour that I am partially responsible for.

Managers need to be aware of how their own behaviour and decisions affect others. Unfortunately, for many managers, 'disobedience' is often a trigger for 'judgement'. But this way of thinking is based on a blind spot, namely the manager's own involvement and the context. One way to examine your own role is to use transactional analysis.

Transactional analysis

Transactional analysis (Steward and Joines, 2010) gives us a tool to learn to see without blinders. It is a valuable way of thinking that makes it easy to incorporate circular vision into your personal leadership. Standard executive behaviour can be explained by transactional analysis and this leads to avoiding inefficiency. Difficulty letting go of tasks that have with real responsibility, falling into repetition, difficulty delegating, doing a lot of extra operational work and difficulty with decision-making can all be tested against it. It can help produce more effective behaviour. In short, transactional analysis is based on the proposition that people can adopt three attitudes during communication: that of parent, child or adult.

The **Parent** in you knows what is right and wrong and how things should be, so he can be critical and condemn, but can also take responsibility and care. The Parent represents the values and norms that you have absorbed since childhood and now use as a framework: everything that your father, your mother, teachers at school, the police, the church, bigger siblings and other authority figures in your life imparted in terms of rules, norms and values is stored in the Parent. Advising, caring, criticising, patronising and authoritarian statements originate in the parent role.

The **Child** represents emotions, life energy, creativity, but can also be dependent or rebellious. The Child pops up whenever you feel or experience something emotional. Communication from the Child role focuses on getting approval and attention from the other person. The Child in us does this by acting obedient (being patient, wanting to please others, being dependent and passive, or a victim) or, on the contrary, by rebelling.

The **Adult** is that part of our personality capable of making considered choices. The adult in us does not allow itself to be driven by childish feelings or parental norms or rules. He registers these things, but is also able to investigate and test. He works with information from external events and examines it internally alongside his current beliefs, norms and feelings. This allows the Adult to make right decisions. The Adult can also source information about his Parent's norms and his Child's feelings. Communication from the adult role is not only guided by (pre-) judgements and feelings.
Aspects of the Adult include questioning, listening, thinking, analysing and gathering information.

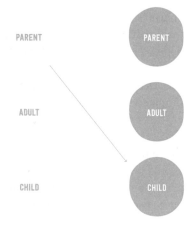

Our own attitude will always influence the other person's reaction. So by being aware of which of the three roles you adopt, you can better guess how the other person will respond. For example, a Parent's communication will nearly always express a command or concern, so the person on the receiving end can rarely react differently than as a Child: 'be good and listen because the boss says so' or rebel against 'those desk guys'. As a manager, you are often tempted to take the Parental role, usually forcing the Child role on the other person.

Michael is a team leader in a chemical company. His team consists of ten highly motivated engineers. He has long been complaining to a colleague that their weekly meeting at two o'clock starts later and later (child role). In the beginning, there were only two latecomers, but now only half of those who are expected turn up by a quarter past two.

Michael can look at this situation in different ways. He could ask why his employees keep coming in late and perhaps draw some conclusions, but instead he thinks the employees are just not putting enough effort into arriving on time. They are too inconsiderate to care, despite the fact that he has raised the issue several times. All the explanations he formulates himself clash with his norms and values. He thus ends up taking the Parent role.

As the problem only got worse, Michael finally decided to simply start the meeting at two o'clock (parent role). The latecomers were shocked and wondered how the meeting could have simply started without everyone present. Michael told them that in future they should just come on time and that sanctions would follow if they kept coming late (parent role). He noticed that the latecomers remained grumpy throughout the meeting (child role), but he thought they would eventually learn their lesson.

This reaction of the staff is an example of the Child role reacting to the Parent role. They feel displeased and misunderstood and can't help but show it. Equally, Michael's parental role could have provoked rebellious behaviour, perhaps even leading to a confrontation. Or the employees could have started laughing among themselves or let themselves be easily distracted during the meeting. This literally 'childish' behaviour is a reaction to this parental role.

When the director calls Michael on the carpet and demands an explanation for the poor quality of meetings (parent role), Michael says that he has done everything he could to get the meetings started on time (child role), but that his staff have "no respect" for his efforts (child role). He becomes angry and says he does not understand why they do not want to cooperate (child role).

In this case, the director assumes the Parent role and Michael assumes the Child role. So everyone has the three positions within them and can use them when interacting with others. As a leader, you can monitor how everyone interacts with everyone else. When you can analyse in which way of being a participant communicates, you can adjust your own communication accordingly. A number of rules apply here:

- When two people, as described above, do not talk to each other from the same role, conflict can arise. We call this a cross transaction (the arrows cross each other).

- Parallel transactions (Parent-Parent, Adult-Adult, Child-Child) usually proceed harmoniously and can go on endlessly. When two people talk to each other from the same role, communication will be good.

- At work, the ideal way to communicate is Adult-to-Adult. There is a free, open exchange of viewpoints and both interlocutors feel heard. Motivated employees communicate in the Adult role. Both employee and manager, client and organisation benefit when talking to each other in such a way that allows everyone to remain in the adult role. To be clear: in the Adult role, there is also room for feelings and authority, but try to keep them as much as possible within the Adult role. Servant-leadership is a way of leading from Adult to Adult.

However, the above guidelines do not mean that, from your Adult role, you can no longer apply norms or values (Parent role) or that you should no longer allow space for feelings (Child role). It only means that it is preferable to communicate such concerns from an Adult role. In Michael's case, he could also have reacted differently in the initial situation.

At the next meeting, Michael says staff behaviour is falling below his yardstick. He asks the latecomers what their reasons are for coming late and how to solve the problem. (Parent communicating from the adult role, circular way)

I find that I get a bit uptight about always waiting for you guys to start the meeting. How can we avoid this? (Child communicating from the adult role, circular way)

If, as in the example above, you see that you and others have fallen into an undesirable pattern of behaviour, discuss it openly with those involved. Learning together how a particular team phenomenon works becomes understanding together as Adults. You can leisurely explore together how to do things differently, and at the same time you make each other constantly aware of the co-responsibility for whatever happens. With circular glasses on, we see that the blind spot in ourselves also blocks change.

LINEAR EXPLANATION

CIRCULAR EXPLANATION

Circular thinking also allows you to evaluate yourself as a servant leader. Because you interact, you constantly influence another person's behaviour. So you can always ask yourself which of the three roles you're occupying when, and in this way explore why the atmosphere in your team is so good at times and why your team members feel comfortable discussing mistakes. But also why your actions sometimes provoke resistance or passivity, and how it is possible to break through those feelings.

To sum up: the circular view assumes that 'working well together' as a team is the result of what happens between people, not what happens in people. It's not our mutual differences that determine our success or failure, but rather how we deal with them. After all, it takes two to tie a knot and two to untangle it. Everyone, especially the manager, has a stake in this. So be curious about your employees' ways of seeing and being and make it possible for them to bring up and help break up unhelpful patterns.

THREE STEPS

1. Defining behaviour perceived as problematic:

- Who does what?
- Causing a problem,
- Against whom?
- And why is this behaviour a problem?
- Only mention specific descriptions of what a person does or says - no reasons or speculations about motives.
- Factual descriptions - not labelling or interpretation.
- Description of the problem - no explanation of what should be done about the problem.
- Can you link this to the Parent-Adult-Child model?

Example
At my team meetings, a moment is often set aside for innovative ideas and suggestions. Every time it becomes as quiet as a mouse; I get no input from my team. The participants look away when I ask them something (Child role). I myself feel the tendency to start preaching (Parent role).

2. Description of solutions so far:

- What solutions have you tried so far?

Example
Provided ideas yourself, referred to ideas from other organisations, asked a lot of questions to prompt for ideas or tried to make them look at other angles.

- What is the common thread in these solutions or, in other words, what are you asserting to yourself or others about what the team should or should not do?

Example

I try to motivate and encourage them to come up with ideas. The other day, I couldn't hold back any longer and told them that I did expect professionals to make a little more effort to come up with suggestions (Parent role).

- Were there any temporary successes in your attempts to solve the problem?

Example

The one time when I was feeling unwell, the output of the brainstorming session was actually remarkably good. And all the ideas came from the team itself.

3. What would the Adult in you do?

- What exactly is the problem you are up against?
- What is the effect of this?
- Do you have a feeling about this?
- So what exactly do you want feedback on?

Example

Colleagues, I notice that - when we get to the point in our meetings about 'innovation' - it often remains quiet. I then start spouting some ideas of my own, but at that point it doesn't feel like we are brainstorming together. When we finish the meeting, I don't experience the sense of satisfaction I usually do after our meetings. How do you experience this? (Adult role)

RECOMMENDATIONS FOR THE SERVANT-LEADER

- Monitor your direction: try to keep the vision alive among your staff (see chapter 1). Be assertive with the yardstick you've set and tough on the outcome.

- Try to look at communication within your team not in a linear but circular way: don't get stuck on individual explanations for employees' behaviour, but examine and discuss with complete transparency patterns of unsatisfactory behaviour and everyone's part in them.

- Be self-critical: dare to reflect on where your part may lie when things are awkward or unclear. It is useful to keep the Parent-Adult-Child model in mind.

3. THE COACH: FOCUS ON COMPETENCE

'The strength of the pack is the wolf, and the strength of the wolf is the pack.'

— *Rudyard Kipling*

Young wolf pups are raised by the whole pack. During their first year, the pups play and receive tutoring from the older members to whom they are regularly entrusted by their parents. For months, the youngsters develop through play and experience, while the other pack members protect them from outside dangers. This growth and development, filled with trial and error, is described  by Packard as a family hunting school where the youngsters are given every opportunity to grow into full and confident members of the pack.

There is a consensus among modern biologists that aggression rarely, if ever, occurs within a wolf pack and that, even when conflicts do occur, they are limited to threats and growls, and almost never lead to a fight. In general, wolves are animals that emphasise their connection with one another, instead of competing. Biologist Rick McIntyre studied wolves in Yellowstone National Park in the United States for 20 years and explained how this behaviour resulted from the strong familial and social bonds that wolves share. No matter how ferocious and resolute wolves can be when defending their pack, they were always gentle and patient towards their young and pack members. He described an alpha male with an impressive physical build who never lost a confrontation with rival wolves, but who, within his own group, liked nothing better than to playfully wrestle with the pups. More than that, what he seemed to enjoy most was to feign losing to the little ones. To McIntyre, this is something that made sense, even to wild animals. For, he argued, "Strength impresses, but it is gentleness we remember best."

In the role of coach, the manager provides:

- Clarity on the formal and informal **roles** of each employee in the team. He encourages team members to develop their innate talents. That way he seeks to improve not only the individual's competence, but also the competence of the whole team.

- **Reflection**, to create a learning environment which doesn't punish mistakes and where, in a relaxed atmosphere, team members can learn from each other together.

DEFINING ROLES BY FOCUSING ON TALENT

One day, the animals of the forest got together and declared: 'We have to found a school. A school for animals to become genuine, complete ANIMALS.' They chose a small group to create a curriculum for the new school.

The committee immediately went to work. The rabbit insisted that 'running' and 'burrowing' be included in the programme. The kestrel thought 'the art of flying' was most important. The carp made it clear that 'silent swimming' should be included and the squirrel made a case for 'climbing up straight trunks of towering trees'. And so it happened.

For the tests, they put the bunny on a high branch and said, "Show us your flying skills. The poor animal jumped, tumbled down, broke his hind leg and got a hole in his head while falling. He was awarded a three out of ten for his clumsy attempt to fly and now that he could not walk very fast, he only got a six for running. The kestrel was asked to dig burrows, like a rabbit. The falcon tried hard, but broke his beak and bruised his wings. As a result, he could hardly fly. He scored four out of ten for his digging skills and could not get more than a five out of 10 for flying due to his injuries. At the end, the committee was surprised that it was the brainless jellyfish who got the best points. After all, she could not break her bones and thus managed to pass all the tests reasonably well. Hurt and disappointed, the other animals dropped out of the school, but not before congratulating the jellyfish on her title as 'most perfect animal'.

(Freely adapted from Toon Tellegen, 1993)

This story demonstrates the difference between competences and talents. Think of competence as an array of expectations in behavioural terms that an organisation demands from its employees. Talent determines the aptitude for a competence.

So a competence is behaviour the organisation wants to see that comes from 'outside' the person because it can be learned and improved, provided the employee has some aptitude or talent for it. For example, the rabbit is competent at 'digging burrows' as a matter of course, but the kestrel, although having very little aptitude for it, can also dig a small burrow. However, it goes without saying that he has no talent for it. We think of talent as something innate in a person. When a talent is displayed, the performer will often not realise how 'unnaturally good' he is at it. Yet it is something a person can learn and develop on their own under the right conditions. The manager can create and influence the conditions in his team. I explain this below in three steps and with the metaphor of a bus. This metaphor comes from Jim Collins (2001), researcher of leadership and author of Good to Great. He puts it this way: as a leader, you are a bus driver. The bus is your team or organisation and the challenge is to get it moving: you decide where you want to go, how you are going to get there and who travels with you.

Collins' research shows that the most effective leaders start by asking who is fit to travel on their bus.

Step I: Recruitment

Servant leaders must be rigorous in choosing who they hire. References, checks, tests and especially interviews help explore whether you can find a potential match. If you don't find a suitable candidate, sometimes the seat is best left empty.

Therefore, it is fundamental that as a manager, you are involved in the hiring of candidates. 'Preliminary work' for recruitment can often be taken up by HR or a recruitment agency, but for the final decision the direct manager must be involved. After all, he has the best insight into the required competences. The management of a medicine manufacturer, for instance, will rarely have a view on who should be hired as a new maintenance technician. However, the foreman, who is confronted with maintenance issues every day, will know the problems that arise on the floor and which specific competences need to be filled. An initial selection should be followed by tests and an interview. For the latter, the STARR method (although designed for recruiters) is a useful tool. The five letters of STARR stand for Situation, Task, Action, Reflection and Result. Using the STARR method forces candidates to give clear and concrete examples of their experience and knowledge. You thus avoid socially acceptable but vague answers. "Are you flexible?" becomes "Give me one specific example where you were challenged on your flexibility in your previous job".

We need to get the most realistic picture of an applicant as possible. For this reason, questions are often asked using the STARR method. When a lie is challenged

by asking for a description of a concrete situation, it suddenly becomes a lot harder to keep lying. Of course, unravelling lies is not the core of the STARR method; the core is the belief that the recent past is the best predictor of future behaviour.

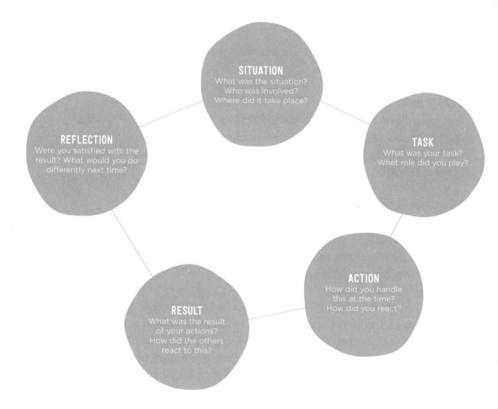

SITUATION
What was the situation?
Who was involved?
Where did it take place?

TASK
What was your task?
What role did you play?

ACTION
How did you handle
this at the time?
How did you react?

RESULT
What was the result
of your actions?
How did the others
react to this?

REFLECTION
Were you satisfied with the
result? What would you do
differently next time?

Properly vetted hiring ensures that employees have been screened for four to seven essential competences. We call these the basic competences, which everyone should have mastered. For instance, a nurse should be able to assemble a syringe and a salesperson should possess a customer-oriented drive. You can expect that as the yardstick or professional standard.

Step II: Talent development

After choosing who is on your bus, you can look at how to grow and cultivate your passengers. For this, it is important that everyone is in the right seat. In classic learning and coaching, organisations focus on developing competence. They often start (unconsciously) from the idea that everyone has to be good at everything. It is only logical that the focus quickly shifts to whatever competences are not well developed in an employee. Often, learning is aimed at eliminating deficits.

In this view, training is seen as a kind of remedy to elevate the employee's skills to a desired level. In itself, there is nothing wrong with this. An organisation should expect certain things and allow employees to learn and develop. However, in practice, all too often we see organisations spending a lot of money on education, coaching and training of competences without knowing whether people have the drive and talent for it. This investment of time and resources is rarely efficient, and can even be counterproductive:

- Managers have to struggle to get people to do things they may have no natural aptitude for.

- Managers often revert to control systems (punishment and reward), for example, to make people do what they are supposed to do.

- A lot of training money is wasted on things that people - unconsciously - have no inner drive for and therefore find it difficult to learn.

A servant leader is particularly attentive to his employee's talents. Therein lies the greatest possible gain for the organisation. Ideally, he guides employees towards areas that fit their personal abilities and preferences, making it easier for them to add value, learn skills faster and simply be happier. You no longer need to motivate them in their performance and development, because you let people do things that fit them naturally. That, of course, is an ideal picture. But for organisations or companies thinking strategically about the future, it's an efficient way of handling learning and development, especially in today's environment that requires people to learn and evolve quickly. You can only achieve this if you make it possible for people to use their talents and not force them to develop competences for which they have little or no aptitude. As a manager, how do you proceed from that base?

The attached figure (after Van IJzendoorn, Van Weert & Müller, 2015) provides some insight. You start from the idea that if you have to push employees to develop a competence they have no aptitude or talent for ('Avoid and don't develop'), this domain is generally best avoided. If you keep hammering the same nail here, you might provoke resistance or even burnout. When in doubt about whether someone fits in this zone, don't hesitate to ask yourself: is this employee cut out for this particular task?

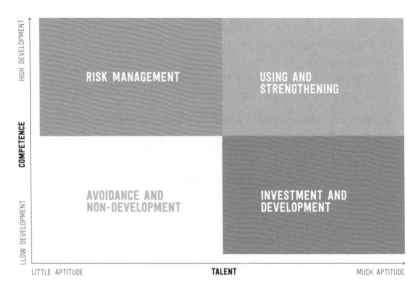

Can tasks that someone really has no aptitude for be redistributed among the team? Is the employee supported with the right tools? A concrete way to discuss this is the method of the Hand (see chapter 5). This way, you can always give someone a chance to reinvent themselves or work with them to find a new role once they regain their strength.

However, if an employee has a reasonable to high competence, but little aptitude ('Risk Management'), you'll have to watch that he doesn't make a mistake. Out of loyalty to the manager or the team, the employee may provide the necessary competence, but he gets absolutely no joy from it himself. The employee shows that he has mastered the competence in terms of knowledge and skills. This does not come naturally because he or she is not intrinsically motivated. In the absence of constant guidance, he is apt to forget or overlook things. This increases the chances of mistakes and dropping out altogether.

If the employee demonstrates a good command of a competency in terms of attitude, knowledge and skills, he is in the quadrant 'Using and strengthening'. The more the employee can make use of that competence, the more successful the organisation will be. When the employee has the right attitude, but he or she lacks the knowledge and skills to be truly successful they come under the heading 'Investment and development'. Investment in education and training will pay off in this case, because the employee has the intrinsic motivation to further develop their competence.

Nathalie recently started working in a clothing shop. Jessica, the shop manager, noticed in the first weeks that she did some things naturally and found others difficult. On the one hand, Nathalie was very easy to deal with and knew how to respond to clients' tastes. She had a gift for selling entire sets of matching clothing, so people regularly bought a shirt, trousers and matching scarf. On the other hand, Jessica noticed that Nathalie sometimes forgot to price the clothes correctly. Clothes were also left lying around in the fitting rooms. Fortunately, she had a timid colleague, Kim, a young man who always arranged the clothes behind her back and corrected the prices. He was glad Nathalie had joined the team, so he didn't have to keep talking to customers. Now he could concentrate on dressing the mannequins on the street-side windows, something he had frequently done in the shop where he worked before. However, Jessica had already noticed that not many customers were enthusiastic about the combinations Kim chose for them, even though they met the usual requirements of colour combinations and fabric choice.

This simple example illustrates how certain traits can end up in the four domains. Of course, the boundaries are not unambiguous and talents or competences are not static concepts, but it is still important to note here that Jessica could make the choice to constantly remind Nathalie to put the clothes away and price them correctly. However, this would give Nathalie less time to deal with customers and deprive her of some of her motivation because she would have to spend a lot more time on things she doesn't really care about. NB: With these four

domains, I don't mean that you should never ask employees to perform a task that doesn't suit them. I only wanted to show that a lot of time and money can be lost when investing in competences that the employees in question have neither a feeling nor talent for. Kim will never become the smoothest salesperson despite countless training courses, and Nathalie will always struggle to reach the top in administration. As a coach, it is therefore essential to look for the talents in your employees and invest in them.

EXERCISE

- Look back at the past year. Think of a specific moment when you felt you were doing well, when you really felt in your groove.

- Describe your experience: what happened? What did you do? Who was there? What did others do? What was the effect on yourself and others?

+

-

TODAY

- What talent did you put to use? What was special about you? Find words to describe this talent.

A view of your own talents (Dewulf, 2012)
Draw a timeline from, say, your first day at work (or earlier; you may choose where you want to start) to today, and run the film from that period in your head: what have you experienced?

1. What were the highs and lows? Moments when you were:

- 'in your element' ... + (or not ... -)?-

- did what you are really good at (or not)?

- were proud of yourself for what you did (or not)?

2. Examine those important peaks and troughs: what did you do? What talents were called upon (or not)?

3. What does this give you in terms of insights into your qualities: what are you good at? What do you derive pleasure from?

4. And what does it say about the context that is important to you? In what kind of environment (role, people, setting ...) did you achieve a good performance? (And where did you fail?)

Step III: Growth, repositioning or dismissal

In the ideal world, all your employees are in the right place, their talents blossom into their full potential and you see them, and therefore your organisation, grow and improve on a daily basis. In some cases, coaching will enable you to better position people, find them a new role or responsibility, allow them the opportunity to develop. However, there are times when you are faced with a long-term mismatch between an employee and the job. When we ask ourselves who benefits from this (the person, the team, the organisation, the client?), the answer may be no one. Intervention is then inevitable and necessary. It goes without saying that dismissing someone is never fun or pleasant, but delaying has a long-term detrimental impact on yourself (and your credibility), your team and the employee in question, who is unhappy because he's in a job that is anything but "right for him".

But again, you can be supportive and gentle on ending the relationship. You can be transparent about the reasons and let him end the partnership with dignity or even guide him towards something new. For instance, people who get off the bus will often later think back with gratitude to the moment when someone made the effort to be honest and transparent, and made him or her feel that the break-up was actually an attempt to let the employee in question 'grow' into a better job. It's worthwhile using such moments as a learning opportunity for yourself and your team. What was missing? What do we need? Who do we look for as a replacement? And so we are back to step I.

EXERCISE

Spend honest and critical time on the following questions:
- Do you have the right people on your bus?

- .Are your people in the right seats?

- Is the seat big enough or does someone need more room to move or more responsibilities?

- Are there people who should get off the bus?

ENCOURAGING REFLECTION IN A COMFORTABLE LEARNING ENVIRONMENT

'There are many people who can say what makes a team play badly; there are few who can say why it plays badly and there are only a few who can say what needs to be done to make it play better.'

— Johan Cruijff, Dutch professional footballer

Important levers to achieve team learning include a strong vision, an ambitious yardstick to judge performance and appropriate support. But what ensures that essential 'learning behaviours' (e.g. discussing work situations, analysing mistakes, giving feedback and asking questions) will occur in your team? The decisive factor in achieving team learning is creating a positive learning environment. But what is that? Or what exactly is it not? According to a sociological study: 'A positive learning climate exists when potential learners regard learning as something attractive or enjoyable, or, in other words, when they assess that there are more advantages than disadvantages to the learning efforts required' (De Rick, Van Valckenborgh & Baert, 2004).

This description shows that willingness and eagerness to learn is mainly a matter of perception. Is learning in our team more likely to be rewarded or more likely to be punished? A fictitious example:

In the preliminary round of an important football cup, a striker is not having his day. He lacks sharpness: he wastes three fine goal chances. The player is doing his best and straining to the limit, but the crowd is merciless: 'Coach, get him off now!'

In an interview after the match, the coach is asked about his rather surprising choice to leave the striker on the pitch. He justified his decision as follows: 'What would have been the effect on his confidence if I took him off after a mistake? And what signal am I sending the rest of the team then? That missing is not allowed? That you then have to pay for that as an individual? This happens all too often in top clubs, but that's not how you create a team.'

Creating a culture together where mistakes are allowed contributes to a strong learning environment. If employees are afraid that a mistake could damage their image, it is difficult to turn awkward situations into learning moments. Employees will, out of concern of coming across as incompetent, uninvolved and negative, be more likely to cover up mistakes or at least not make them open to discussion.

When team members are imbued with the idea that making mistakes is necessary, they will learn more easily. After all, as with children we want to encourage their development.

Where the custom was for each child to come to the master or teacher to have their drink bottles opened, we put some bottle openers on a table and taught them to open a bottle. And they succeeded, except for the occasional mishap. As a teacher, you have to be prepared to take that in. In this way, pupils become - even if only slightly – more independent, more self-reliant.
(Jeroen Reumers, primary school teacher, Rotselaar)

Too often in teams, mistakes are punished or ignored. Now and then they give rise to a further tightening of the rules or procedures. But that means there is no error analysis, and that hinders the learning process. In the long run, people might no longer dare to experiment, or they might start hiding their mistakes. This is diametrically opposed to learning. Together with your team, find a good balance between controlling and preventing risks and a healthy tolerance for mistakes.

Karim has been working in a household products distribution centre for only a few weeks. His job is to collect customer orders on pallets with his forklift. Karim still works significantly slower than his colleagues. He wants to do his best and then sometimes he feels a bit rushed. A while back, out of nervousness, he dropped a box of washing powder. The box tore. In all candour, he reported this to foreman Rick. The latter was not at all understanding: 'That's the last time, buddy! Next time, you pay for it yourself.'

Indeed, it is the last time Rick will catch Karim at fault. At the next mishap, Karim's behaviour will leave one guessing. He will try to cover up his mistake or blame it on someone else. A coach, on the other hand, encourages learning and supports his employees' thought processes. He develops competences, at individual and team level. He creates the ideal preconditions for learning, individually and from each other. That way, Karim might have had the following reaction to his report of the torn wash powder box:

'Cool man, that you came to tell me. Don't worry about the box. I know from my early years on the job that you are still building up a routine. So it's perfectly normal for things to sometimes go wrong. What just happened? Do you have any idea how to prevent it next time?'

Another thing that can help create a positive learning climate can be found in how the leader acts. What the team leader does or does not do will greatly influence his employees' perceptions of a psychologically safe zone and the desire to learn. Does the manager make himself vulnerable? Does he admit his own mistakes? Does he offer them up to discussion? Can he look at himself critically?

Charlie is headmaster of a primary school. When a teacher is ill, he likes to step in. He enjoys keeping in touch with the profession, being in front of the classroom. At four o'clock, he plops down on a chair in the teachers' room and starts talking.

'What a day! My timing left much to be desired. It started with the maths lesson. I wanted to teach the children exactly what 'the average' means. It seemed like a good idea to let them experience it themselves, so I took them to the playground. Everyone ran the hundred metres. Anna timed them and Matt noted down the times. It never occurred to me that this could take quite a while. On top of that, it suddenly started raining and blowing, turning everything into chaos. We rushed back to the classroom and before I knew it, the children had to go to gym class. Without me having had the chance to make my point ...'

When the manager lets his team know that he too makes mistakes, he sends an important signal to employees: we all make mistakes and we can all learn from them together. A coach who seems to be 'perfect' is handicapped because it doesn't help him build an effective learning environment.

EXERCISE

- Think about your team. When was the last time you had a meaningful learning moment together?

- How did your team members react the last time someone made a mistake?

Learning, or failing to learn, is driven by the individual's attitude. If someone is convinced that mistakes are learning opportunities, he will behave differently from a person who believes that admitting mistakes will later be used against him.

As your team members constantly interact, exchange experiences and unconsciously influence one another, a shared idea of what they consider normal, good or important emerges. This collection of attitudes, assumptions, beliefs and values is your team culture. Faster than you think, 'undesirable' beliefs can creep in and nestle inside it. To achieve the kind of learning culture you want, say what you do and do what you say. For instance, you can preach open communication while unconsciously responding defensively to any criticism or feedback from your employees. A culture in which every mistake is openly punished rarely leads to good results.

There are five monkeys in a cage. At the very top hangs a delicious bunch of fresh bananas. Every time the monkeys try to climb the steps up to the bananas, they get drenched in a blast of cold water. After a while, the monkeys give up and stop climbing the steps. Then a monkey from the original group is replaced by a new one. Every time that monkey makes an attempt to grab the bananas, it is stopped by the four 'original' monkeys because they don't want to get wet too. The new monkey conforms and no longer tries to go up the steps. After a while, a second monkey from the original group is swapped with a new monkey. There are now three original monkeys, one who has conformed and one new monkey. The new monkey smells the bananas and wants to climb the steps, but is stopped by the three original monkeys as well as the conformed monkey. After a while, the new monkey too conforms and does not try to climb up to the bananas. So it goes on, until there are five monkeys in a cage with steps to a bunch of bananas and yet no monkey dares to take the initiative to grab the bananas. And all this without ever having been punished themselves.
(Source: unknown)

You can easily apply the above example to a workplace. Someone on the floor takes an initiative that was not in good taste, even though it was well intentioned. He is fired and his replacement asks his colleagues what he should look out for in his new job. They, of course, tell him that he should not take any initiatives. This, of course, is what he will say to the next new worker and so on. Before you know it, a culture has formed where newcomers are advised against coming up with initiatives to improve their work, for fear of being fired. Obviously, this is not a very efficient working environment. Be sure to make mistakes a subject you can discuss rather than penalizing them outright.

EXERCISE

- List beliefs that you think make sense for learning, e.g.: giving each other feedback is a gift because you are giving someone a learning opportunity.

- What views does the team have about addressing one another about desirable as well as unwanted behaviour, or on giving each other critical feedback?

RECOMMENDATIONS FOR THE COACH

- Seek out your employees' talents and try to apply them accordingly. Don't expect that 'everyone should be able to do everything'. There is nothing more unequal than treating everyone equally.

- Never penalize mistakes mercilessly. Consider them as an inevitable part of learning.

- Dare to be open and vulnerable about your own mistakes. This can help create an open atmosphere where feedback and dialogue become the norm.

IN CONCLUSION

Throughout Part I, we have examined the importance of vision. This is the direction you want your organisation to go and the basis from which you can develop bold ideals for the future. A shared vision creates bonding between employees and the organisation.

Next you fix a yardstick to judge your employees' behaviour and results. When you notice that they are not measuring up, you provide support. This support will always follow the same four steps: addressing - expressing - discussing - agreeing.

For support, you can act from three different roles: as a manager, as a leader and as a coach. It is here that you really make a difference in meeting the ABC needs of your employees. In the overview, you can see how the three positions are linked to the ABC.

The leader	The organisation		ABC of the employee
THE MANAGER wants ...	to give **space** by steering for results	to guide the **flow** of activities	in furthering **autonomy**, he wants employees to take responsibility and to decide for themselves how to tackle things
THE LEADER wants ...	to give **direction** and guard the vision	to strengthen **relationships**	in furthering **bonding**, he wants to contribute to meaningful goals in a good atmosphere.
THE COACH wants ...	to determine **roles** by focusing on talent	to stimulate **reflection** in a safe learning climate	in furthering **competence**, he wants employees to be good at something and be appreciated for it.

I return one last time to the metaphor of the wolf pack. The alpha male allows space to his pack members to make their own decisions and go their own way, but ensures they are moving forward efficiently in the right direction, taking into account both internal and external factors. He indicates the right way by leading or communicating with his gaze because he understands the importance of communication within the group. He will rarely be aggressive towards members of his pack, and is assertive only when he needs to be. He tries, along with all members, to nurture and grow the young into the best version of themselves. The alpha wolf understands that the pack is his family, that he needs them, just as the pack needs him. As Rudyard Kipling wrote: 'The wolf depends on the pack, and the pack depends on the wolf.' Always keep this framework in mind as a leader.

That's as far as the comparison with wolves goes. In Part II, I delve further into the three different roles of the manager. It covers the four styles of a manager, the five characteristics of a servant leader and the six competences of a coach.

SERVANT-LEADERSHIP IN FOCUS

The concept of servant-leadership can easily be summarised in the following image. We try to capture the complexity of a team in a simple diagram: a sphere with four layers. When all four layers are in harmony, we speak of a team in drive. When this is not the case, something is not running smoothly somewhere in one of these layers. The beauty of the image is that these four layers not only apply to team dynamics, but also to individuals, managers, colleagues and even the entire organisation.

The top three layers of the sphere teach us that a team can fulfil a vision with enthusiasm when members...

Stand together behind a vision they truly share.
When the the vision is concrete and balanced with support when needed. When work is organised in such a way that we all feel a hundred-per-cent motivated.

Yet the key to a team's success lies in the fourth and final layer: confidence.

It is important to understand that too much control or guidance goes against the attitude of connection and trust, even though it can sometimes conflict with our natural tendency towards control. At the same time, letting go of authority does not mean leaving everything to chance. The right balance lies between these two extremes: an optimal tension between distance and closeness. When colleagues come up with proposals, initiatives, or ideas, we find that we have be able to stand back and let them get on with it. This allows our colleagues' creative potential to be maximised.

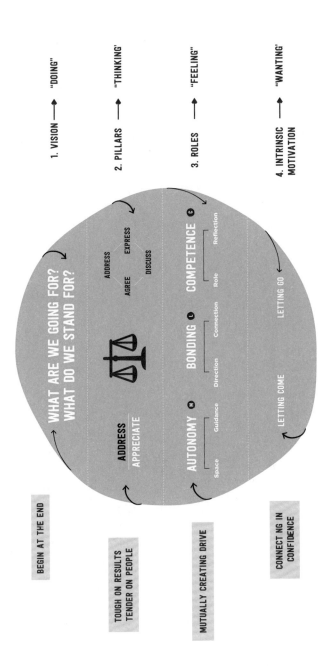

1. VISION ⟶ "DOING"

2. PILLARS ⟶ "THINKING"

3. ROLES ⟶ "FEELING"

4. INTRINSIC MOTIVATION ⟶ "WANTING"

WHAT ARE WE GOING FOR?
WHAT DO WE STAND FOR?

ADDRESS
EXPRESS
AGREE
DISCUSS

ADDRESS
APPRECIATE

AUTONOMY ⓜ   BONDING ⓛ   COMPETENCE ⓒ

Space   Guidance   Direction   Connection   Role   Reflection

LETTING COME   LETTING GO

BEGIN AT THE END

TOUGH ON RESULTS
TENDER ON PEOPLE

MUTUALLY CREATING DRIVE

CONNECTING IN
CONFIDENCE

PART 2

DEEPENING YOUR UNDER-STANDING

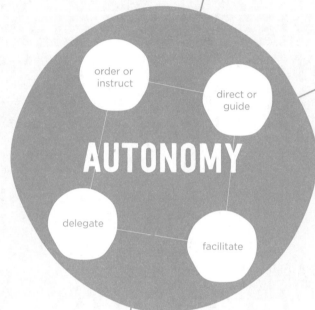

order or
instruct

direct or
guide

AUTONOMY

delegate

facilitate

FOUR STYLES
OF **MANAGING**

FOUR STYLES OF A MANAGER

'A lot of what we call management consists of making it harder for people to work.'

— Peter F. Drucker – management consultant

1. FOUR STYLES TO GUIDE YOUR EMPLOYEES TOWARDS AUTONOMY

In this chapter, I zoom in further on your role as a manager and introduce you to situational management, developed by Paul Hersey and Kenneth Blanchard (1977). I base this chapter on their concepts and add my own interpretation of them. The premise is that the ideal style of management is best tailored to each specific situation and the level of competence of your individual employees in relation to a specific task. By observing your employees' behaviour and adapting your own behaviour accordingly, you as a manager will be better able to respond to your employees' needs in a specific situation. The end goal is to guide your employees or team towards autonomy and self-management, because that is the desire of both the employees and the manager. By way of introduction, let's look at the following example.

Do you remember the day you learned to drive? You were probably excited that first time you put the key in the ignition and heard the car roar. You were an enthusiastic beginner and needed clear instructions from your driving instructor (competency level 1).

Most likely, you also remember well the first moments of frustration. The car stalled time and again or your headlights lit up as you tried to turn on your indicators. Perhaps you wondered how on earth you could ever pass that driving test. You had reached the disillusioned learner stage and although you had mastered the basics of driving, you still needed some extra guidance (competency level 2).

Once you could drive smoothly and received one compliment after another from your instructor, your self-confidence grew along with your ability. And just when you were starting to feel a little more confident, you still fell silent once in a while. At that point, you were a capable but cautious driver who still needed support (competency level 3).

Eventually, you get to the point where the car seems like an extension of your body. You can now drive a car without even thinking about it. You are now truly a 'self-driving professional' and no longer need guidance (competency level 4).

This example illustrates how each competency level and each situation requires different behaviour from the leader or manager. Depending on the situation, a specific management style will serve your employee better. This will lead to a better result than if you as a leader continuously adhere to one particular style.

So, first of all, it is important to look at what the employee needs to be able to perform a task: for instance, an employee starting something new is likely to need some more instructions rather than maximum autonomy. He wants clear explanations on how to do something. The essence of situational management is to adapt your management style to your employees' level of competence in a given task and that you aim to let them work as independently as possible over time

So the trick will be to challenge employees on the one hand and encourage development of their skills on the other. The interaction between the degree of challenge and the level of development will bring out varying moods in the employee.

The attached diagram shows the mindset a person may be in while performing a task or activity. It is determined by 'Challenges' and 'Skills', which are contrasted.

Specifically, this diagram (Csikszentmihalyi, 2007) represents the state of mind an employee is in when performing a task. These feelings are determined by the interaction between the challenge you see in a task and the skills you will need to meet this challenge. If there is very little skill and little challenge, we end up with indifference. If there is a great challenge but little skill, then the employee will worry about how to complete the project. If, however, there is a great skill and a great

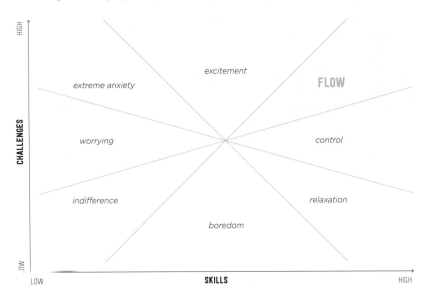

challenge, then we arrive at the most effective and enjoyable way of working. The experience in this way of working is called flow (Csikszentmihalyi, 2007).

EXERCISE ON FLOW

Task 1

Do you remember an actual work situation from the last few months when you could be totally absorbed in your occupation? You were so focused that:

- you might have forgotten the time for a moment;
- you experienced a sense of happiness, satisfaction or relaxation;
- you were quite proud of yourself.

Task 2

Think of an example where you brought your employees into a flow. Did you do this by making the challenge greater or lesser, or by improving their skills?

How do we treat our employees to as many moments of flow as possible? To achieve this, we will have to be able to adapt our management style to the employees' competence level each time. Could it be that expectations are not clear? Does someone need a more intensive moment of guidance? Does he just need a nudge? Or does he really just need more autonomy and responsibility to perform a task with motivation?

FOUR STYLES OF SUPPORTING YOUR EMPLOYEES

Situational management is based on two assumptions. The first is that employees want to develop themselves and prefer to do their work as independently as possible provided they are given the necessary support. The second is that the 'ideal leadership style' does not exist, but that your effectiveness is highly dependent on whether your style is adapted to what your employees or the situation require at that moment.

There are four styles for this: instructing/instructing, directing/supporting, facilitating and delegating. These phases are brought together in the diagram based on two dimensions: the instrutional or task-oriented dimension and the supportive dimension.
Both dimensions will always occur together, but depending on the management style, the focus is more on one dimension or the other. Based on the adage 'soft on people, hard for results', the servant manager should always consider what his employee needs in a given context to perform a task properly. After all, the manager and the employee are jointly responsible for that. As a manager, you should ask yourself t wo questions:

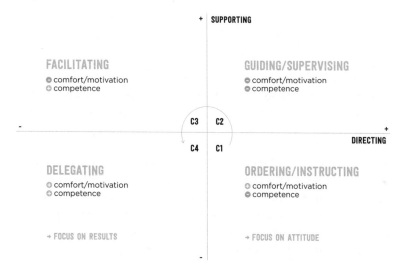

1. Does my employee need direction?

This refers to the extent to which a manager is involved in the content of the task: how much he needs to specify exactly what the employee should do and what his responsibility is. How much he instructs where, when and how the task should be performed, and monitors the outcome and performance.

2. Does my employee need support?

This is about the extent to which a manager takes the employee by the hand, uses the personal touch, encourages, is helpful in solving problems that arise in task performance, promotes mutual cooperation and involves the employee in decision-making.

Competence level 1 (ordering/instructing)

Little support - lots of direction

> *Jeff is working his first day in a copy shop. The intention is that he would eventually be able to run the shop independently, but that is too much for now. First of all, someone has to explain to him in detail how all the machines work, how to work the till, how to prepare quotes, and so on.*

Detailed instructions (instruction cards, checklists and so on) and close monitoring of task performance can help Jeff here. The supervisor then accurately spells out what, how, when and where tasks should be performed.

This style is best suited for an employee who needs to learn a new task. He is excited to start the task, but is not yet competent and unsure whether he will do it well. This can occur with both new employees and employees who have been working in an organisation for some time but are given new tasks and responsibilities. In such cases, there is a need for clear instruction, demonstration, explanation.

Ordering is the authoritarian brother of 'instructing'. After all, sometimes certain arrangements are fixed and it is crystal clear what is OK or not OK. Setting a yardstick and articulating expected behaviour are important in this. It can help here to keep the balance between the two pillars in mind: making your expectations clearly explicit while offering support. You can do this even in your authoritarian role. Just remember to consider your employee's point of view.

'Jeff, when I arrived, I saw you in front of the entrance to our copy shop. We agreed not to do this because it doesn't look very professional to customers. I would like us to stick to this agreement and for you to take your smoking break at the back of the garden. Okay?'

In busy times, the situation often demands that 'orders' are given out quickly and there is no time to worry about the employee's feelings. Keeping things on an adult level, it can sometimes be better to come back to it later.

'When I asked this morning for those 150 folders for our biggest customer to be delivered asap, I was so adamant because I think it is important that the customer with the highest priority gets good service.'

A concern with this style is that applying it to an employee who has outgrown this level of competence may be perceived as 'mothering'. Think back to the parent-child pattern of communication. Employees might feel patronised as a result.

Competence level 2 (guiding/supervising)

Lots of support - lots of direction

By now, Jeff knows the basics of all the machines and can deal with everyday customers without difficulty. Still, his boss stays with him in the shop and guides him with regular customers who have special requirements and need to be prioritised. The boss says a lot of things, such as how posters and restaurant menus are of great importance to traders. He considers Jeff's new proposal to sell a loyalty card for daily visitors, but still occasionally corrects him. For instance, he insists that Jeff would be better off using the cash register's shortcut keys during busy periods to reduce waiting times.

Explanation of job content is still very important in this style, but now it also involves a high degree of guidance to implement the norms in practice. Understanding as well as motivation is important for performance. So the manager continues to give instructions and closely monitor performance, and he also explains decisions, asks for suggestions and rewards progress. Above all, he will be attentive to the employee and actively listen, consult and involve him, compliment and encourage him. For example, the employee is asked to think about suggestions to solve problems and discuss these with the supervisor. If the employee is properly supervised, he gains success experiences in this phase and can gradually be left to take care of things on his own.

The supervisory style can be perceived as patronising when the employee is monitored for too long and too closely. This can also be seen as pampering, while being very time-consuming for the supervisor. For the manager, it is then important to take further steps in letting go and increasing the employee's autonomy.

Competence level 3 (facilitating)

Lots of support - little direction

It is his first day alone in the copy shop and Jeff is excited. He chooses his own music and feels that by now he has found a balance between regular customers and passers-by. Every day his boss stops by before and after closing time and also regularly between hours. He is curious if Jeff has any questions, but the latter confidently shakes his head. Jeff has generally mastered the job.

Still, there are sometimes situations where he is taken out of his comfort zone, during very busy end-of-year periods when the shop is flooded

with students. His boss listens to him with curiosity, discusses what is
going wrong, gives him some tips (e.g. he could ask the students to
email him their final papers so that he can better plan out his work) and
asks if Jeff is happy with that.

The supervisor acts as a stimulator, a sounding board, and assists the employee on request. Manager and employee decide together how the work will be done. To adopt this facilitation style, the employee must be competent enough to handle the task.

In this style, it may be challenging for the manager to still hand off the tasks and not take over (again). However, it may work better in the long run to be curious about the employee's concerns and let him think along with you about how the task should be done. As a manager, you can then express your confidence about the task going well. You can then stand behind your employee and serve as a back support until the employee begins to do the job well on his own.

This facilitation style involves an employee at competency level 3. The employee can perform tasks well, he has the right skills for them, but he is still sometimes uncertain - he does not think he can handle a situation or occasionally gets out of his comfort zone. Or else, he does not want to do something for whatever reason (he does not see the point, he does not consider it his job, etc.).

A problem with this style is that employees who are in fact ready to do the task completely on their own may experience a lack of confidence in their ability. Or that the employee in need of guidance and coaching becomes insecure while already cycling through the job without 'training wheels'.

Little support - little direction

After six months, Jeff knows the ins and outs of the copy shop. He orders ink himself, calls the mechanics when a machine falters and even manages to convince some casual customers to commit to the shop. His boss comes to the shop for a few minutes every fortnight to go through the output together and set criteria for certain tasks. Thus, they agree on a maximum budget, paper thickness and delivery times, and Jeff can look for a new paper supplier based on those requirements.

Most employees are eventually willing and capable enough to complete tasks successfully, and these come to bear the responsibility for decision-making and problem-solving at this level. For this, they are given the necessary authority. The manager monitors the criteria for getting the task done well, without determining the 'how'. So there is some support from the boss, because he will still want to know if there were any problems or, during the process, he may want to know about the state of the planning and execution. In addition, the supervisor will occasionally want to provide information about plans proposed or imposed from the organisation. The manager releases 'the how' of the task and thereby expresses his confidence in his employees, to help them perform tasks properly. Responsibility for operational excellence thus lies entirely with the employees.

From control to self-management

As presented above, you could interpret the model in a linear way: 'Employee X does such and such, so as a manager I should deal with it in such a way.' Of course, it is not that simple. Situational management becomes effective only when the desire to serve, to increase your employees' self-direction, precedes it.

Thus, the servant manager will constantly examine whether he is effectively providing the support his employees need. If you do not test your thought process around the right management style, if you as a manager are therefore the thinker and the employee merely a passive object, it can lead to increased dependency in the employee. This brings us back to the parent-child relationship, and the tension and friction that can accompany it. Servant management is not something you do for your people, but with them, from one adult to another. Situational management means trying to assess every situation without bias. Check regularly with the employee whether you are helping him correctly, or to see what the situation requires. The following reactions from an employee may occur:

- I don't quite get it yet. Can you explain and show it to me one more time? (C1)

- Will you stay with me when I do it independently the first time (C2)?

- I think it will work, but can I call you if I get stuck? (C3)

- I can manage if you tell me which criteria the result should meet. (C4)

Other factors can also help you determine the choice of leadership style. As a manager, your own experience, your ability to switch between the different styles, your preferred style, the way you want to be led and so on, all play a role. But the task itself, its importance and urgency also determine which style you will use. And then there is the employee who may require a certain style because it suits his self-image or because he was so used to it with your predecessor.

In my view, managing has more to do with a serving and facilitating attitude towards your employees than with rules of conduct. More to do with what you as a person are in your work and life, than with handy tricks or behaviour according to specific rules. Servant managers want to contribute to the development of others.

Leadership, in other words, involves continuous learning. The skills needed for any style can be learned through self-reflection and training. The main source for this kind of learning will be found in the feedback you get from your employees.

EXERCISE

Think of a work situation where you supported your employee with the right style. Make the link to situational management:

- What was the competency level of the employee?
- What style did you approach the employee with?

Think of a situation where what you did didn't have the desired effect.

- What was the competency level of the employee?
- What style did you approach the employee with?

Think of tasks you now assign, supervise or support.

- What competency level do you think your employee has reached?
- What can you change in your behaviour to allow the employee to progress to the next level?
- Which style of leadership suits this employee (instruct, guide, consult or delegate)?
- To discover your own preferred style, complete the 'situational management' test on this book's website (www.servant-leadership.world).

2. FOUR STYLES TO GUIDE YOUR TEAM TOWARDS AUTONOMY

In this section, we look for the most effective way to manage teams. To do so, we use the different phases in group development as described by Ten Hoedt, Tuckman and Jensen (1977). We link these phases to the well-known principles of situational leadership (Hersey & Blanchard, 1977), incorporating the ideas around servant management to influence teams towards increasing autonomy and self-management. The practical example below illustrates the difference in maturity of teams and their degree of self-management.

This is a great example:
Home care and district nursing in the Netherlands underwent years of mergers, upscaling and associated efficiency exercises. The pyramid became wider and higher. This brought numerous bureaucratic effects. Tasks became increasingly specialised. For example, planners were hired to provide district nurses with a daily diary, optimising the route from patient to patient. Patient calls were answered by call centres. Standard times were set for each type of intervention in an electronic timekeeping system: for example, 10 minutes for injections or 15 minutes for showering. This could then be conveniently linked to the billing system. To reduce costs, these different treatments (called products) were categorised according to level of training, to save costs; for example, a higher-educated nurse did not have to do work that could also be done by a carer. The long-term effect of this bureaucratisation was that the system thus lost sight of the end user as a human being. The teams with once-motivated care staff no longer experienced autonomy and scope for volition in their jobs. They gradually alienated themselves from their patients and from their own work.

In response, the non-profit organisation Buurtzorg was founded in 2006 by Jos de Blok and a team of district nurses. The teams consist of 10 to

12 people with each team serving 50 patients in a small, defined area. They do intake, planning, schedules for holidays, days off and administration entirely themselves. Care is no longer cut up into different 'tasks'. The teams decide where to rent an office and what it should look like. They decide how best to integrate into the local community, which doctors and pharmacists they need and how best to collaborate with local hospitals. They decide when to meet, how to divide tasks among themselves, if and when to expand or split their team. They monitor their own performance and decide on corrective measures if productivity drops. There is no leader and important decisions are taken collectively. However, they do have a coach (without any decision-making mandate) whom they can call in if they cannot manage on their own. The vocation and vision of care staff and the raison d'être of home care were thus restored to their purest meaning: the well-being of the patient takes precedence over the organisation's own interests or 'survival instinct'.

The results have been astonishing. Buurtzorg has since become the largest neighbourhood organisation in the Netherlands (with some 8,000 staff). A 2009 study by Ernst & Young proves that Buurtzorg costs on average almost 40 per cent fewer care hours per client than other care organisations, and yet employees say they can finally take the time for a chat with patients again. That employees appreciate this is shown by the fact that Buurtzorg has been named 'Best Employer of the Netherlands' no less than three times (in 2001, 2012 and 2014) (research by Effectory and Intermediair). It functions as an international example of how an organisation can work with self-directed teams (Laloux, 2015).

Becoming the best employer may sound like an appealing idea. And the link with self-managing teams is quickly made here. There are numerous examples of self-management in other sectors: manufacturing companies, ICT, consulting firms, schools, media companies and the food industry. The main question will therefore be how to implement these principles of far-reaching self-management in your own organisation.

If you want to increase self-direction in your team, it is important to understand the following: whether it is a team of salespeople, accountants, designers, engineers or teachers, a team does not become result-oriented and independent automatically. Indeed, one might conclude from the case of Buurtzorg that even if you start implementing the principles of self-direction tomorrow, transforming a bundle of individuals into a team, and then into a team with high self-direction does not happen overnight. Experience shows that a team may feel somewhat let down on the road to self-direction by the leader's coaching attitude. The leader then becomes disappointed by the team's lack of initiative and discipline. The team is frustrated because they suddenly have to figure out everything themselves and don't know how to do it. To avoid this, we will have to master the art of guiding the process, beginning with individual interactions. Unless - as in the example of Buurtzorg - you can start from scratch and lay out all-new structures staffed by new people, this will be a gradual process. In the next section, we will look at how to carry out this process with the team you already have.

SITUATIONAL MANAGEMENT OF TEAMS

A team operation is not simply the sum of individual members' contributions. I define a team here as a group of people who depend on each other to achieve a collective ambition. Within it, there is a constant mutual influence that creates a dynamic partnership. These dynamics are characterised by different phases. The way in which the process passes through these phases determines group performance and the degree of autonomy it can achieve. The model of situational management, developed by Hersey & Blanchard (1986), is consistent with the theory of group development by Tuckman and Jensen (1977):

1. **Forming** (formation of the group) Members take a wait-and-see attitude. There is no group feeling yet and individual positions and roles have not yet been determined.

2. **Storming** (the conflict phase) In this phase, members try to establish their roles within the group. This inevitably leads to conflict when ideas of team members are at odds with each other.

3. **Norming** (the norms or standards phase) The rules and methods of cooperation are determined. Common team goals are defined and shared. The important and less important roles are defined. Collaboration can begin.

4. **Performing** (performance phase) The group becomes a team. Team members complement each other. People work harmoniously towards the common goal.

HIGHT	MIDDLE		LOW
T04	T03	T02	T01

← DEVELOPED ————————————————————————— IN DEVELOPMENT →

T01 LOW COMPETENCE/STRONG COMMITMENT
T02 SOME COMPETENCE/WEAK COMMITMENT
T03 HIGH COMPETENCE/VARYING COMMITMENT
T04 TO4 HIGH COMPETENCE/STRONG COMMITMENT

Again, situational management is based on the relationship between, on the one hand, the task- and relationship-orientation of the manager and, on the other hand, the development level of group members with regard to specific tasks. Just as the model of managing individual employees starts from their development level for one particular task, one can speak of the development level of the group with respect to a particular task. These team development (TO) levels are scaled from TO1 (low) to TO4 (high) and relate to both team competence and commitment. This scale changes as the task changes. As with the individual employee, the manager of the team will also have to learn to lead the team flexibly (handling different styles) as well as effectively (handling the right style at the relevant group stage).

Style 1 ORDERING/INSTRUCTING/ and phase 1 FORMING

In the model of situational management, the first style is 'instructing/ directing'. The manager exhibits a lot of task-oriented and little relationship-oriented behaviour. Indeed, in the Forming phase, group members are willing but not competent to perform the task as a group (TO1). The manager can speed up the completion of this phase by setting a clear goal for the group and defining the measuring stick together.

It is important to give sufficient attention to individual group members. This can be done by clearly communicating expectations regarding task content and performance. The supervisor will also closely monitor task performance. The guidance offered provides the safety that group members need. The instruction offered by the supervisor gives the group the chance to solve dependency problems in this phase, thus stimulating the group towards greater task orientation.

Style 2 DIRECTING/GUIDING and phase 2 STORMING

In the Storming phase, there is already some group competence (TO2) and so the manager needs to lead differently. There is growing competence, but willingness to take on tasks is lower than in the previous phase. Besides task-related guidance, there is a need for more explanation and clarification of assignments. There is room to ask questions about content and a lot of energy is put into giving support and encouragement.

The recurring conflicts always make this phase the most critical. It is of utmost importance for the manager and for the team and individual team members to handle these conflicts well, in order to create opportunities for growth. Conflicts that get out of hand create chaos, while the suppression of conflicts can lead to apathy among team members. The manager will challenge the team to resolve conflicts in a regular and structured manner. In this phase, the manager will combine an active and guiding attitude with constant explanation and motivation, including on conflict management.

Style 3 FACILITATING and phase 3 NORMING

The development level of the team is now quite high (TO3). The group members have the skills needed to perform the task but they are still too uncertain or not always ready to perform the task independently. A lot of support from the manager in the form of encouraging input is crucial. The leader promotes and supports the efforts of group members in carrying out tasks and he shares decision-making responsibility with them. Common group feeling will increase and the emphasis is on openness and harmony. This phase can be accelerated and influenced by raising values and norms explicitly within the group as a leader.

Group unity is strengthened by encouraging integration, involvement and speaking thoughts out loud. Less direction on the manager's part facilitates the voicing of opinions and enables open conversation. Working together is perceived as realistic and achievable. The team can already solve many problems by itself, with limited support from the manager.

Style 4 DELEGATING and phase 4 PERFORMING

The responsibility for decision-making and problem-solving lies with the group. Indeed, the group has arrived at a developmental level (TO4) where it can handle both relational and task-oriented issues.
Team members are looking for improvements to increase performance, individually and as a team. This phase sees a lot of personal growth among team members. There is room for recognising the individual needs of team members and a desire to work together to ensure that each team member achieves results with the help of the others.
Group performance is constantly under discussion, but always in a very open, constructive atmosphere. The leader challenges by providing future vision.

The team can deal effectively with changing organisational conditions, so it can be referred to as a self-learning team. This also means a marked reduction in the number of blind spots within the team. The manager can transfer responsibility for decision-making and problem-solving to the team. Creating optimal framework conditions, bringing in knowledge, negotiating with the wider organisation and so on will henceforth be the main tasks of the manager.

	RELATIONSHIPS	LEADERSHIP
FORMING	Unfamiliar, uncertain, tense	• Uncontested • Giving instructions, indicating goals • Task-oriented, less relation ship-oriented • Direction by manager gives peace of mind
STORMING	Bonding on the basis of similar opinions: coalitions and conflicts as important feature = seeking one's own place, which leads to profiling oneself in a certain field: conflict. Moreover, one's chosen place is not always the most constructive	• Position of power becomes position of authority from now on • Leader must 'earn' his place by distinguishing himself in an area that is necessary/desirable for the group members. If not, leadership is questioned • Leader as conflict coach
NORMING	• Recognition of opinions, capabilities and skills of group members • Differences are seen as added value • Group develops its own values and norm • !Risk: complacency, stagnation due to insufficient challenges	• Encourage critical sense • Invite to experiment, push boundaries • Create space for group members to be allowed to make mistakes • Explicitly discuss values and norms • Encourage commitment
REFORMING (SELF-LEARNING TEAM)	• Not individual but group performance is the norm • Intervening in each other's work is the norm • Mutual relationships are sufficiently clarified: communication is mainly about improvements in work • Sometimes (temporary) relapse	• Responsibility for decision-' making and problem definition is shared • Developing vision for the future • Evaluating group performance • Creating preconditions • Bringing in new knowledge • Negotiating with the organisation

EXERCISE

You can make an analysis of your own management style on this book's website.

FINALLY

Let me note here that, again, there is no 'best' leadership style for teams. What is more important is that the leadership style employed suits the team's stage of development, because this leadership style can influence the team's development process either positively or negatively. It should also be clear that the group process is a process of mutual influence. It takes place between all members of the group. It is not possible not to participate in the process. The manager is aware that he is part of the group and thus participates in the group process. What a manager does and does not do, what he says and withholds, is involved in the process. This implies that a manager has to 'earn' his position during the various stages of the group process. A formal appointment as a leader will not suffice: after the Forming phase, the leader will have to be able to translate his position of power into a position of authority. In reality, this means that in the perception of the team members, the leader will possess a number of capabilities that they consider necessary to achieve group goals. If the manager does not have these capabilities, he will come under pressure to change his role. In a lot of organisations, the manager can invoke formal power resources in this case and still remain in place. The consequences of this are the blocking of the group process and group development. This is certainly not what we expect from leadership. Therefore, from its vision of effective leadership, an organisation may certainly set a yardstick when it comes to self-reflection and self-knowledge on the part of the manager.

RECOMMENDATIONS ON THE FOUR MANAGERIAL STYLES:

- Be aware of the development opportunities of your employees and your team. Strive to guide them towards greater independence.

- During this process, try to focus mainly on your own influence. How can you adapt your style to the competence level of your employee or your team?

- Consider this model as a way to explore in dialogue what the employee needs to perform a task as independently as possible, without feeling 'thrown in at the deep end'.
  Therefore, regularly probe the needs of your employee and your team.

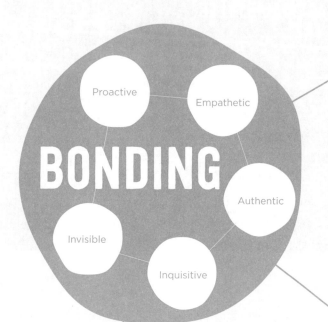

FIVE CHARACTERISTICS
OF A **SERVANT-LEADER**

FIVE CHARACTERISTICS OF A SERVANT-LEADER

IIn the previous four chapters, I outlined frameworks that the servant-leader can employ. The image of the shepherd illustrates what we mean by servant-leadership:

The shepherd does not 'lead' in the sense that he stands in front of the group. He herds his flock from the back. It is the sheep in front who act as the eyes and ears of the organisation. The shepherd knows which direction they are going (vision), knows how fast he wants to get there (yardstick) and makes sure he chooses the least steep mountain paths that run alongside running water so the flock can rest (support). He alternates between three positions to lead his flock. In addition, he also adopts different styles. For instance, he herds the lambs differently from the older more experienced animals, as they already know the way.

In this chapter, I explore which characteristics make someone a servant leader. After all, you can also have a vision, use a yardstick and steer a team in a particular direction without necessarily being a servant-leader. Even non-servant leaders can switch between the positions of leader, manager and coach, or use the four managerial styles as a technique. So what makes a servant leader unique? What are the traits that characterise him?

What distinguishes the servant leader is his ability to be tough on results and soft on people. These two facets combine nicely in the workings of a piano. The original name for this instrument was pianoforte, because it could be played both hard (forte) and soft (piano). It is precisely this combination that makes the servant leader effective. The servant leader is tough on results. He will safeguard professional standards and take into account five domains:

- **F**unctioning of the employee
- **O**verview
- **R**esults
- **T**ime monitoring
- **E**valuating

Because the servant leader believes that he can achieve hard results only when he is soft on people, he will put himself at the service of the ABC needs of employees. Therefore, these five traits characterise the servant leader:

1. **P**roactive. The leader looks ahead and prepares for future developments.

2. **E**mpathetic. The leader is empathetic towards his employees and tries to see things from their point of view.

3. **A**uthentic. During learning processes, the leader remains himself. He will be consistent, honest and truthful.

4. **C**urious. Because of his authentic and empathetic attitude, the leader is curious about his employees. He looks for their drives and qualities.

5. **I**nvisible. A servant-leader strives to make himself as unobtrusive as possible, in order to be increasingly proactive, profound and innovative.

Throughout this book, I've covered several ways a manager can be tough on results: monitoring the vision and employing a yardstick to judge your employees' performance, following up closely, prioritising the right results and making it clear within what time frame they must be achieved. Afterwards, you evaluate these steps together with your team, looking for improvement. In this chapter, I delve deeper into the equally important characteristics of the servant-leader, by elaborating on how to be proactive, empathetic, authentic, curious and invisible.

1. PROACTIVE: KEEP TO THE MAIN THING, THE MAIN THING

'You can't change the direction of the wind, but you can change the position of the sails.'

— H. Jackson Brown

PROACTIVE

John is the CEO of a large packaging firm. He is often too busy, which is the case again today. He employs two receptionists, Rita and Sandra, who for the first time in two years take leave on the same day. And as John's desk is right next to the reception desk, he feels he has no choice but to take over their work. He takes phone calls, receives the paper supplier, speaks to visitors and tries to do his own work in between.

The above example shows that having a busy schedule does not necessarily mean effective leadership. In this example, John is like a captain of a large ship, scrubbing the deck. The ship has no captain at that moment. Inevitably, this means that things on his agenda are taking precedence that, as CEO, are not necessarily important.

As a manager, you too may experience constant 'pressure' on the job. In periods of stress, when you are juggling tasks and deadlines, it isn't easy to keep your focus on what is really important in the long-term and the effects that will generate sustainable success. To maintain control of your own schedule and your organisation or team, it is important to think about your own time management: that you are proactive and engage as much as possible where you, in your unique role, can make a difference. A first step is to become aware of the difference between things you can and cannot influence.

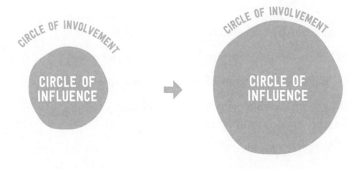

The circle of involvement and the circle of influence (Covey, 1989) offer clarity here. Within the circle of involvement are the things that affect and impact us, but over which we ourselves have little or no control. Big or little things like the weather, traffic jams, pressures at work, poor organisation, unclear agreements, unspoken feedback, and so on become big energy guzzlers that we cannot avoid. These things are frustrating and can throw you off track.

The circle of influence refers to things you can actually influence - your own plans and goals, your dealings with colleagues, friends and superiors, your outlook, the time you put into important things, your own development, and so on. Often our attention is taken up by the circle of involvement. But instead of focusing your attention and energy on what you can't do anything about - troublesome colleagues, traffic jams on the way to work, rain on the day of your outdoor team building exercise, and so on - I invite

you to explore the circle of influence. Where do you have influence? However small your influence may be, this is an opportunity to be effective. By focusing your attention and energy here, you end up expanding your circle of influence. For problems where we have no influence at all, we can only try to resolve inwardly. For instance, we can decide to accept an unwanted situation and give up resisting it.

EXERCISE 1

- Which bottlenecks are important to me right now?
- Where is this problem situated within the two circles?
- On which part of the problem do you have direct influence?
- On a problem where you depend on others,
  do you have any indirect influence?
- What can't you change?
- Look at the situation again, but from your circle of influence.
  How can you begin to enlarge your circle of influence?
  Start from small things that are within your reach.
- Direct influence?
- Indirect influence?
- What difference would this make?
- Based on this assignment, what concrete action
  can you take in the coming week?
- What support do you need for this (from colleagues,
  manager, HR) and how will you obtain it?

EXERCISE 2

Decide with your team which things you no longer want to pay attention
to because you can't influence them anyway. Then determine together
which activities you do want to pay more attention to.

KEEP TO THE MAIN THING, THE MAIN THING

'Urgent matters are rarely important and important matters are rarely urgent.'

— Dwight D. Eisenhower

John has too much on his mind. All his multitasking and sense of urgency leave him stressed. He feels rushed and so his reactions are often short-tempered and tense. He feels resistance from people around him, which saps his energy and leaves him even more tense. This turns into a vicious circle. He lacks detachment and so becomes even more stressed.

Being too busy often indicates a lack of focus. Yet 'being busy' often seems to be socially valued more than working in a relaxed drive. I advocate abandoning the belief that being busy should be the norm. Replace it with well-balanced time management. Increasing your circle of influence in a proactive way raises questions about time allocation and planning.

John survived the day and was able to keep the situation under control by putting out fires here and there. He quietly decides to take a proactive approach the following day and asks Rita and Sandra to agree to schedule their future days off to ensure that one of them is at reception at all times.

You can take every available servant-leadership training course in existence, but if you don't set priorities for yourself, it won't make much difference in the workplace. Servant-leadership is about the fundamental choice to sow first to reap later, to pay attention to your relationships with and the development of your employees, to anticipate difficulties, to network and innovate. To make those choices, it can help to understand the tension between time and priority. If you have never considered time management as a manager, chances are that your prioritisation looks like this: urgent matters take priority over non-urgent matters. But besides urgent, you can also consider what is important (see the attached chart by Covey, 1989).

	URGENT	NOT URGENT
IMPORTANT	Firefighting Urgent problems Deadlines	Preparation Clarification of values Planning Building relationships Empowerment
UNIMPORTANT	Interruptions Some reports Some meetings Many so-called urgent matters Many popular pursuits	Inconsequential matters Wasting time Some phone calls

To clarify what character a task has (in which of the four quadrants it belongs), you can ask yourself the same question four times, but with a different intonation each time. The basic question is: should I do this now? With the four quadrants, you can always emphasise which of the words makes it clear to you which kind of task it actually is. You will see that twice you will get a positive answer and twice a negative answer. It is of utmost importance that, as a servant leader, you try to be as proactive as possible, that you have things under control and that you are prepared. If you are working reactively all the time, you aren't really a leader; you are little more than a victim of your environment.

Quadrant 1 - urgent and important
Should I do this now?
Yes, it is unavoidable.

Quadrant 1 is about work you need to do immediately to prevent problems. It is often clear what this includes: solving all kinds of acute problems, complaints, projects with a short-term deadline and sometimes firefighting. It often jams up our schedule, but it is also fun work that often brings quick and considerable satisfaction.

But that is also the risk: before you know it, you spend all day dealing with urgent matters that are only a small part of your job. These can be caused by the poor planning by others, or are really unimportant things that are presented by others as urgent; they can also be things that you have neglected and that have now grown into a crisis. If you are not careful, more and more jobs will end up in Quadrant 1 and you won't get around to doing anything but putting out fires. With every urgent job, pause for a moment and ask yourself:

- Is this urgent or can it wait a while so I can
  finish what I am working on now?

- If it is urgent, is it really my job to solve the problem?

Quadrant 2 - not urgent, but important
Should I do this now?
No, but you have to do it later.

This is the quadrant of proactivity. In quadrant 2, you will find the things that are important, but are not (yet) under time pressure. If you leave them for too long, they become urgent. Eventually you will make them happen, but the risk is that something of great importance will be done too hastily. Here lies the basis for servant-leadership. After all, it is in this quadrant where you can live your vision, do talent management, where you can plan and improve, where there is room for development and learning. You can also search for structural solutions to recurring problems that force you to put out fires. By spending time in quadrant 2, you avoid tasks from this quadrant flowing into quadrant 1. It is here where you have to make sure that you remain proactive as a manager and do not become merely reactive.

Quadrant 3 - urgent, but unimportant
Should I do this now?
No. Someone else has to do this.

John gets interrupted every so often or called or emailed about issues that he really shouldn't have to deal with. Perhaps you've had people coming to you with a problem, expecting you to solve it. In themselves, these issues may be very urgent and need to be dealt with. However, the question is whether, from your view of your role as a manager, you should deal with the issue yourself. You can delegate the tasks that you've placed in quadrant 3. Not to get rid of them, but to guard that you can best occupy your three main roles and not make your team dependent on you by taking on jobs they can do themselves.

If you are not conscious of this, there is a good chance that you will end up taking on all sorts of extra tasks that will conflict with your priorities for serving long-term goals and the team. Conclusion: invest in quadrants 1 and 2. Be aware that 'urgent' weighs down quadrant 2 and so you can delegate things that are not important from your position as a manager (quadrant 3).

Quadrant 4 - not urgent and not important
Should I do this now?
No. Try to avoid this.

Useless newsletters and surveys, checking your e-mail every five minutes or scrolling through Facebook: quadrant 4 is best avoided as much as possible. You could call this the 'escape quadrant' – what you do if you don't feel like doing your job or don't have clear goals. If you find yourself spending too much time in quadrant 4, it is important to ask yourself and your co-workers how your commitment relates to your responsibility.

The four quadrants can be reduced to a metaphor. If you take a glass jar and fill it with a few large stones, the jar appears full. However, if you pour in a handful of gravel, it turns out there is actually quite a lot of space left. If you then add a handful of sand, it will also fit. Finally, if you pour some water into the jar, that fits, too. But if you had started the other way round, first the water, then the sand and then the gravel, the stones would never have fit. The big stones represent quadrant 2 activities: the things that are important but not urgent. Plan those first and only then can you start filling in or avoiding the rest (e.g. quadrant 4).

EXERCISE

Every task, no matter how small, takes time. Draw two axes to form important and unimportant and urgent and non-urgent quadrants. Write down activities that you spent more than 15 minutes on in the past month. Which belong in which quadrant?

Complete the priority matrix below. Based on this layout, you can schedule, delete, delegate tasks, and so on.

Write down all your activities in two columns: time-savers and time-wasters, and divide these again into two columns: factors you can influence and factors outside yourself.

TEAM EXERCISE

List the team activities that belong in the circle of influence. Discuss together how you can give priority to activities that are important, without neglecting urgent issues. This way, you make your team a participant and co-owner of your time management.

EXERCISE

You can use the quadrants in different ways. Consider during your (working) day: am I now working in quadrant 1, 2, 3 or 4? This will immediately give you an insight into your tasks and disruptions.

| TIME WASTERS | | TIME SAVERS |
WITHIN MY INFLUENCE	OUTSIDE MY INFLUENCE	WITHIN MY INFLUENCE
Self-discipline, procrastination	Obligations/too many meetings	Prepare well for meetings (an agenda)/ only meet if it's really necessary/ establish a time limit
Assertiveness	Unexpected visits	During certain tasks, shut your door
Concentration	E-mail	Go through E-mails once in the morning, once in the afternoon
Unclear division of tasks	Colleagues	Keep your archive and your folder structure up to date; find a system that is clear to everyone and make sure everyone adheres to it
Unclear objectives	TTelephone calls	Let someone else pick up the phone
Lack of planning	Crises	Consult regularly with colleagues/ employees; monitor the division of tasks
Poor organisation	Sickness	Put goals on paper and make an action plan
Not delegating	TTasks coming to you from quadrant3	Learn to say no

| TIME WASTERS | | TIME SAVERS |
WITHIN MY INFLUENCE	OUTSIDE MY INFLUENCE	WITHIN MY INFLUENCE

2. EMPATHETIC: KNOW EACH OTHER'S MANUAL

'The sage is compassionate, therefore he can be demanding. He is sober, therefore he can be magnanimous. He does not stand above others, therefore he can be authoritative.'

– Lao-Tzu, Chinese philosopher

EMPATHY

If you have worked in different organisations, teams or positions yourself, you may have already noticed that a different version of you is addressed or evoked each time. Sometimes you may have felt not fully appreciated or that your ambitions were ignored. Sometimes you gained confidence and felt you were realizing your full potential. Sometimes you were bothered by issues in the job that were never discussed. Sometimes you were glad that your supervisor gave you development opportunities.

To systematically engage with employees on these issues, many professional organisations have a coaching cycle with a recruitment interview, planning interview, performance interview, adjustment interview and sometimes an evaluation interview as well. While management and employees usually see the point of doing these interviews, they also sometimes perceive them as an annoying interruption to their real work (quadrant 1). Yet it is crucial to systematically keep a finger on the pulse of employees, because it is precisely their individual qualities and ambitions that make the difference (quadrant 2). The growth of employees will help determine the growth of the organisation.

In truth, everyone is responsible for their own development, but that does not mean an employee cannot be guided and mentored during the interview process. The basis for this is laid out in the annual performance evaluation, a key way of maintaining the cooperation that brings out the best version of your employees, and ensures a good match between each person and his function or role in the organisation.

In most cases, a supervisor and employee each bring two agenda items to the performance review. In my experience, the topics they discuss are all too often minor problems or concerns about the content of the job itself. They are less about cooperation, well-being or development. Also, the boundaries within an evaluation interview are not always clear to the employee. On top of that, people don't always start the conversation well prepared.

To make performance conversations truly worthwhile, connecting collaborative or growth conversations, I have developed a methodology to facilitate the conversation: the methodology of the hand. It is based on two principles: first, the purpose of the conversation should be to get to know each other's 'operation manual'. Here, it is important that employee and manager enter into a conversation from equal positions, in order to come to non-committal agreements together. The second principle is that people often have a better view of their problems and shortcomings than of their strengths and talents, although that is where the greatest area for growth lies. The methodology will therefore have to provide room for discussing successes, for drawing attention to talent together and for those moments when the employee is seriously motivated.

You can use the methodology of the hand to prepare a growth conversation with your employee. The aim is to identify six themes together: strengths, ambitions, resistances, connection, development and support. It is also important to know how the employee perceives your leadership. These themes correspond to the symbolism of the fingers of the hand. Each time the employee speaks and you as manager listen, you ask questions and contribute to the conversation. With the vision and the yardstick in mind, you try to come up with SMART agreements together that will make a difference in practice. Each should try to name facts as concisely and concretely as possible. The most concrete question is therefore always at the top.

	EMPLOYEE	MANAGER
Thumb (strengths)	• What for you were one or more moments in the past year that you are proud of or especially satisfied with? • What are you good at? • What are your qualities? • What do you enjoy in your job? • What can you delight in? • What makes you enjoy your job? • What can you contribute to the team? • Are we leaving any of your talents untapped?	• What is your employee good at? • What qualities does he have? • What does he delight in? • When do you see him flourishing? • What does he contribute to the team? • What can you learn from him?
Forefinger (ambitions)	• What specific projects or objectives do you envisage for the coming year? • When will you look back on this with satisfaction? • What do you need to still be working here happily in 10 years time? • How do you see yourself evolving? • What are your goals? • How do you expect to achieve them? • Have you found a good work-life balance? • How do you see this evolving?	• What is the employee's ambition? • Where do you see him in a few years' time? • Where does he see himself then? • What goals does he set first and how does he want to achieve them? • What goals do you set for him?
Middle finger (resistance)	• Name one or more things we can do to improve our work. • What would you like to change in your job? • How can this evolve positively? • Are there things that bother you, and what do you think could be done about them? • What would be a reason for you to leave us?	• What would you miss the most if you no longer worked here? • Why do you want to stay with us? • What do you find important in working together? • What gives you confidence in the organisation? • What values do you and the organisation share? Are your ideals still the same as when you joined us? • How do you feel towards your colleagues?

Ring finger (bonding)	• What would you miss the most if you no longer worked here? • Why do you want to stay with us? • What do you find important in working together? • What gives you confidence in the organisation? • What values do you and the organisation share? Are your ideals still the same as when you joined us? • How do you feel towards your colleagues?	• What would your employee miss most if he no longer worked with your organisation? • Why does he want to stay with your organisation? • What values do we share? • What appeals to him about our vision?
Pinky (development)	• What are your difficult or weak sides? • What competences, skills, or knowledge do you want to develop further? • Where do you feel you still need to grow? • What will you work on? What are you less good at? • What training do you need?	• In which way do your employees still want to grow? • What are their weaknesses? • What competences and skills do they want to develop further?
Palm (support)	• Prepare three tips that can help me lead you better or to grow in my role as a manager. • What can I do differently, more of, or better? • Do I sometimes ask too much of you? • Do you wish for more explanations, support, or coaching? • Do you think our cooperation is going well? • Do you think you are appreciated for your talents?	• How do you think you can further develop as a manager? • What do you think your employees have lacked in the past year in terms of leadership, management, or coaching? What can you suggest to improve this?- • Are there team solutions that would include more shared leadership? • What would you miss the most

In practice, I find that the hand method reduces the reluctance to discuss issues around cooperation, well-being and development and to clear the way for agreements on these issues.

The appreciative approach provides a robust start to the conversation. The majority of your employees do most of their tasks to contribute to the team or for the sake of excellence, right? And what you give attention to, grows. The forward-looking and constructive continuation symbolized by the index finger allows building on what the employee is already good at. By the time you reach the middle finger, the tone has been set and an atmosphere of transparency, appreciation and comfort has been created. The employee understands the objective of the conversation: getting to know each other's operation manual. He owns the conversation: after all, it is about his manual. He has an overview of the structure of the conversation. All this helps to ensure that both employee and manager can start the conversation well prepared. This makes the hand method not only simple and lively, but also very effective.

EXERCISE

A template to prepare (for the employee and for the manager) for this conversation can be downloaded from the website accompanying this book. This way, you can breathe new life into your next performance review.

3. AUTHENTIC: BE TRUE TO YOURSELF

'You are born to be original. Don't die a copy.'

— John Mason

What is authenticity? When is someone authentic? The answers to these questions are always vague, broad and incomplete. This time will be no different. Claiming that something like authenticity can be learned from a book is like claiming that you could learn to play the violin just by reading scores. The curious thing, however, is that although no one is able to define authenticity, it is nevertheless, I believe, a key characteristic of a 'true' servant leader. I will make an attempt to discuss some of the principles an authentic leader wants to act upon.

AUTHENTICITY IN PRACTICE = TRANSPARENCY

In my view, being authentic has to do with 'staying close to yourself'. By this I mean that you can try to really listen to yourself at all times and be transparent about it to other people. It is a lifelong, unfinished project of introspection and reflection. There is some truth in the statement that someone who wants to lead must first be able to lead themselves. A leader is first and foremost 'curious' about his own thoughts, feelings and needs. He listens to himself thoroughly in the first place. He follows his gut and uses his mind; it is absolutely essential to want to know who you are or where you want to be, what you stand for, and what your core values are.

Here, it is useful to reflect on your own accumulated stock of beliefs. After all, your actions result from thought patterns that you hold, consciously or unconsciously. So the way you think about an event will determine your behaviour (IJzermans, 2009).

> Jesse and Jasmine are 11 years old. On a hot summer afternoon in August, they are playing on the beach in Ostend. They decide to go for a dip. They are both waist-deep in the sea when a big wave suddenly comes at them (event). Jasmine thinks of the adventure film Cast Away (thought), which she was watching with their dad and exclaims with delight: 'This is exciting!' Jesse, on the other hand, has clearly remembered Mum lovingly but sternly saying in the car: 'I don't want you to go deeper into the water than your waist. If a big wave comes, it could be really dangerous' (thought). Jasmine happily jumps into the wave (behaviour), Jesse takes no chances and quickly runs back towards the beach (behaviour).

- Events
- Thoughts
- Feelings/behaviour

An event often gives rise to a particular belief, which triggers a feeling and/or leads to certain behaviour. These beliefs often derive from previous experiences.

> In an insurance company, director Chris insists during every meeting that everyone must be at work by 8.30am. That way, they can get calmly prepared to spend the day at the counter receiving customers. It is his belief that this is the only way to get the job done right. After all, customers are already at the counter by nine o'clock.

This example shows that beliefs are 'instruments' by which a person relates to the world. Knowing that a belief is created and moulded by certain experiences, fears or needs already tells us something about the relative value of its 'truthfulness'. It is clear that Chris's deeper motive is his concern that the insurance company continues to run well, and he is anxious that if this condition (the belief that everyone should be present at 8.30am) is not met, work will be compromised. Chances are that

Chris has had some experiences in his own upbringing or career that triggered this conviction. In those specific cases, that conviction may also have been 'true'. It made sense to relate it to those situations at the time. But that does not make it transferable to all other situations. It can be interesting to examine your own (unconscious) beliefs too, without necessarily having to modify them. A belief in itself is neither good nor bad. You will find that there are helping and hindering beliefs. When the person in question suffers from a situation because of a hindering belief, we can examine this belief together.

An authentic leader tries to examine his beliefs and motivations, and from there, what he actually feels, thinks and thinks about in the current situation. In this way, he will avoid acting without really thinking from his emotions (child role) or from his normative beliefs (parent role). Authenticity in this form is strongly linked to the adult role: listening to what is going on inside you and understanding where it originated, in full transparency.

THE POWER OF VULNERABILITY

At the same time, this awareness allows an authentic leader the space to be vulnerable. In a nutshell, we could say that leaders who are not authentic often unconsciously try to make the uncertain certain. Ideas, plans, assignments and so on are presented with great firmness based on the idea that this is what is expected of a good leader. It follows that little space is allowed for discussion or dialogue, because discussion and dialogue can make the leader vulnerable. Authenticity, however, has nothing to do with being right or being proven right. When people insist on being right, it is often driven by fear that by being wrong, they will also lose a part of themselves. An authentic leader realises that he is in a constant learning process and that 'being wrong' is part of this. To allow this, vulnerability is inevitable.

At the next meeting two employees say that it is difficult for them to be present at 8.30 am because they have to drop their children off at school. But they will always be there before nine and serve the first customers without any stress.

It may remain Chris's belief that this is unacceptable, but then he would lock himself into his beliefs. However, when he reflects to himself what his real concern and fear is, he could be transparent about it to his staff. Through this transparency, the two staff members will also be challenged in their adult roles to understand Chris's rationale, to find ways to reassure him and come to an agreement together.

INTEGRITY: DOING WHAT YOU SAY AND SAYING WHAT YOU DO

Keeping commitments, transparency about what is going on in the organisation and honesty are important aspects that the manager will adhere to in order to be a good servant-leader. The authentic leader is reliable and credible. He keeps his word, says what he does and does what he says. Chris himself will not be able to be late too often because he will lose credibility. Actions speak louder than words ...

The importance of harmony arises in all areas. Acting authentically towards your environment also means being true to your own personality and core values. In behaviour, it means feeling, thinking and acting are all in accord. It is the cornerstone from which an authentic person tries to be in constant dialogue with the world and an authentic leader of his employees. Being authentic with your employees and your team is not a sleight of hand, but rather a life attitude.

Although the above is only an incomplete summary of what authenticity means, it does reveal that servant-leadership is linked to authentic leadership. But authenticity starts with you, of course. Only by staying true to yourself can you grow into an authentic leader. The exercise below therefore addresses important questions: what moves you as a person? What are you trying to realise and experience deep inside yourself? If you clarify that and consciously choose to do so, you can be open to others and help them in turn find and realise their individuality. That seems to me to be the deeper meaning of working together. It then becomes living together.

MISSION: ALWAYS BE YOURSELF

Everyone's behaviour (including your behaviour as a manager) is influenced not only by the environment (such as your team), but also by inner factors. What you can do, how you think about something, who you are and what motivates you, largely determines what you do in which context. You could therefore argue that the success rate of a venture/goal/project becomes exponentially much higher when it is embedded in a person's beliefs, identity and sense of purpose. Therefore, the task below is very important to increase the effectiveness of your leadership (Dilts, 2008).

Through this awareness, you grow as a personality. It is, as it were, a tool for reflecting on your behaviour. In doing so, feel free to act as if you have reached your goal, even if you don't yet know the exact details of your goal.

The environment: what's going on?
Your leadership takes place in your team, in your organisation. Suppose you want to become a servant leader in your own personal way.

Name those environmental factors of your team and your organisation that you will need to consider:

	SUPPORTING FACTORS	CHALLENGING FACTORS
TEAM		
ORGANISATION		

Behaviour: what am I doing?

You have taken the context into account. Now you can flesh out your goals. What new behaviours will you exhibit as a servant leader?

Skills: how do I do it?

In setting your goals, you can identify what capacities ~ skills you have and others you still need to develop to achieve your goals. What capacities and skills do you employ as a servant leader?

Beliefs: why am I doing it this way?

What are your personal thoughts and beliefs about servant-leadership?

Identity: who am I really?

Everyone has their own identity. This is all about your core. When someone makes their identity known or it comes through in their behaviour, it has the most impact. Identity resonates through all layers. The combination of your main beliefs that make you you shape your vision. List the most important ones. This is your personal credo.

Mission: why am I doing it?

Here it is about understanding those principles, values and norms that are essential to you. What you understand them to mean is up to you. You have given your own interpretation to it: for example, the principle of forgiving people or putting love at the centre of your life ...
An example of a leader's mission statement might be: 'By providing servant-leadership, I put the people at work at the centre and, as a leader, I work towards developing independently responsible employees and independently responsible teams.'

4. BE CURIOUS: DISCOVER YOUR CORE QUALITIES

'Everyone has talent: if you judge a fish on its ability to climb a tree it will live its whole life believing it is stupid.'

– Einstein

CURIOSITY

A very important characteristic of a servant leader is that he is genuinely curious about what is going on with his employees. I already mentioned in Chapter 3 that a servant leader is someone who takes a circular view of communication. This means that we are constantly mutually influencing each other in our social interaction. As a servant leader, you survey your team and your role within it as if from a helicopter.

The servant-leader seeks to understand before he wants to be understood (Covey, 1989). It is a constant task for him not to fall into interpreting other's actions, but to be curious about the 'why' behind his employees' behaviour. This sounds easier said than done, but Ofman's (2015) methodology can help you with this.

The servant leader is curious. He sees his team members working together, excelling, discussing or achieving results. As he looks at his employees' behaviour by way of circular vision, aware of our constant mutual influence he is also curious to discover where this behaviour comes from.

Cecille is a secondary school principal. Two years ago, she hired Sarah, a young biology teacher who knows no limits. Sarah wants everyone in the staff room to meet on weekends or give the school a makeover during holidays. She also signs up for every extracurricular activity, even when there is no specific role in it for her.

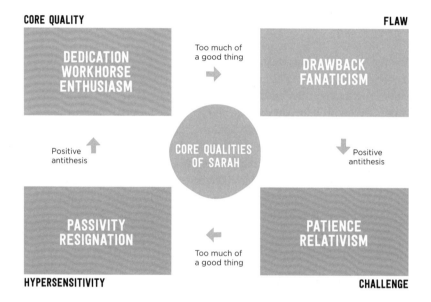

CORE QUALITY   FLAW

DEDICATION
WORKHORSE   Too much of
ENTHUSIASM   a good thing   DRAWBACK
                                ➡   FANATICISM

                    ↑   CORE QUALITIES
Positive   OF SARAH   ↓ Positive
antithesis   antithesis

PASSIVITY   PATIENCE
RESIGNATION   ⬅   RELATIVISM
                          Too much of
                          a good thing

HYPERSENSITIVITY   CHALLENGE

Core qualities are traits deep inside a person. They are the specific strengths that characterise a person par excellence. Everyone has some of these qualities or talents. These qualities are so intertwined with a person's identity that they are always present. In Sarah's case, her core qualities are dedication and enthusiasm. Occasionally core qualities are not gauged correctly. When core qualities are too dominant they can become a flaw, as in 'overdoing' it. Sarah's core quality of enthusiasm could turn into fanaticism.

With this flaw, Sarah's biggest challenge can be surmised. Someone who is fanatical and driven will have a hard time putting things into perspective, and standing back to carefully consider a situation. This is something Sarah can work on, though. Wherever her shortcomings lie, there will be opposing traits that can lead to the opposite extreme. Being too patient or reflective could lead to passivity or resignation, traits that contrast sharply with her core qualities of decisiveness, enthusiasm and dedication. The core quadrant brings this structure into focus.

Even when you sense resistance from employees, a core quadrant is a good way to gain insight into the situation. Think back to the last time you had a conflict with someone. At the height of the conflict, the other person probably saw you as being mostly 'negative': shouting, expressing yourself emotionally, sulking, ignoring, ... Yet, at the same time you were preoccupied with things that were very important to you: your colleague (supervisor, partner, friend, child) 'should finally understand that ...' or 'be reconciled with ...'. So in your eyes, you were doing positively intended things. Behind the negative form of expression were commitment and dedication to the relationship.

It may sound strange at first, but behind every resistance, behind every negative behaviour, there is a need. This also applies to your employees. When they express themselves negatively, it actually means that they do not see something they 'want' (positive) to happen, or that they want to preserve something they have. As a servant leader, it is essential to harness their resistance to find out the underlying need. Start by no longer regarding difficult behaviour as resistance, but rather as awkward communication. And as circular vision tells us: everyone is involved in that communication and therefore equally responsible for the 'solution'.

After a while, other teachers report to Cecille that Sarah reacts rather nastily when they do not agree to her plans. Sometimes Sarah lets slip that she 'has to do everything herself' or that 'the others are not behaving in a professional manner'. This creates tensions in the staff room, as the other teachers do try to sign up for the extracurricular activities that they need to be involved in, but without compromising their personal lives. The teachers call Sarah fanatical and perhaps obsessed. And they say she resents them for not sharing her over-the-top commitment.

Ideally, what the servant-leader will do is examine the difficult behaviour (in this case, Sarah's toxic comments) in terms of awkward communication.

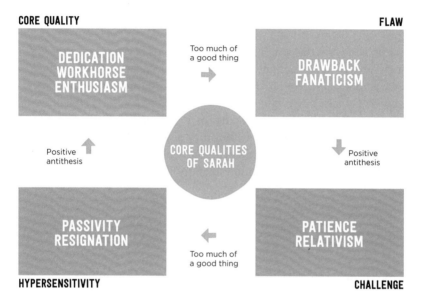

Valuing someone's core quadrant will lead you, as a manager, not to readily label anyone. You won't start by seeing Sarah as someone who is fanatical or pushy, but by learning to understand that behaviour like hers stems from a quality or unfulfilled desire and gets

triggered in a particular context. After all, Sarah's nasty comments are nothing more than an expression of her frustration that not everyone shares her unbridled enthusiasm.

It will be counterproductive to address Sarah on her flaws ('You shouldn't be so fanatical', 'You come across as pushy to the other teachers'). It is much more effective to explore together the need behind her behaviour, so that the behaviour ceases to be 'undesirable' and becomes just 'awkward communication'.

Cecille takes Sarah aside to discuss the situation: 'I really appreciate your efforts, and I notice that you also make great efforts to involve the other teachers in all your initiatives. However, to them it sometimes seems like you blame them for not being able to attend everything all the time. Is that true?

We do not doubt the commitment of staff we hired with great care. We highlight that commitment even for those who have lost sight of their own commitment a bit. And then we start talking about the effects of how that commitment is communicated. In this way, the 'problem' becomes coachable, because instead of a 'character flaw' we have made it a 'communication problem'. Informing people about the effects of their behaviour and making them accountable for it yields much better results than giving well-meaning advice related to their attitude and personality.

EXERCISE

Think of an employee and consider his flaws or shortcomings. Be curious about his underlying core quality. Try to fill in the four quadrants.

TIP Of course, you can also do this assignment with your employee. Then work on concrete examples, so that it becomes clearer how his qualities or flaws emerge during work and where possible challenges lie. It goes without saying that a core quadrant is not static, and can vary with the context, how you feel, which people you interact with, and so on. Consider these nuances in focus when asking for examples.

Possible questions that might help as you reflect along with the other person:

• Quality: What do I appreciate in my colleague?

• Flaw: Why am I sometimes annoyed with my colleague?

- Challenge: You could really start doing this (more).

- Hypersensitivity: Which colleagues' behaviours sometimes make you unhappy?

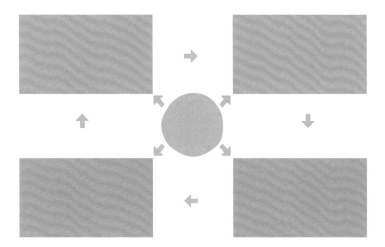

Core quadrants also offer an illuminating view of lingering tensions and conflicts that arise between people or between colleagues. Indeed, these conflicts are often caused by the fact that colleagues' qualities and flaws are difficult to reconcile.

Things seem to be calming down, yet John (an experienced, older teacher) still regularly complains to Cecille about Sarah. He certainly does his bit, but has always been subdued and thoughtful rather than a showy extrovert. When Cecille calls both of them to her office to discuss the conflict, they seem diametrically opposed. Sarah says John is 'lazy', where John accuses Sarah of being 'pushy'.

In such cases, it is useful to draw up a combined core quadrant so that the contradictions are clearly highlighted. In terms of qualities or flaws, John and Sarah are 'hypersensitive' to each other's behaviour.

This means that traits of the other person are at odds with their own qualities. The core quadrant can lead people to recognise their own part of the problem and thus reframe the conflict. Future friction can be avoided if the two parties are willing to take more account of each other's sensitivities. Once both people are made aware of this, it will create clarity all round, which may not have been possible before, because 'the other is too stubborn to change anyway'.

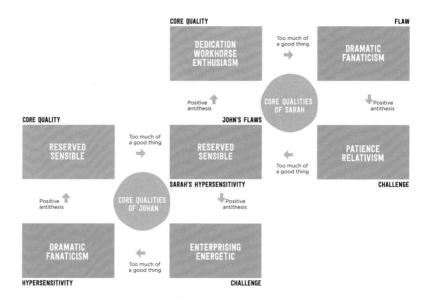

5. INVISIBLE: CREATE NEW LEADERS, NOT FOLLOWERS

'The goal towards which parents have to strive in relation to their children is this: to make themselves superfluous.'

— P.H. Ritter, writer and journalist, 1882-1962

DIt is no accident that this book begins with the example of a parent teaching his child to ride a bicycle. As a parent, you wish your child only one thing: that he will be able to stand on his own two feet, make his own decisions and face the challenges that come his way as a mature and resilient human being.

We recognise a servant leader by his employees: they grow. To encourage their growth, the manager systematically grants them more powers while investing in their development. Granting powers ensures that employees develop a proactive attitude and self-confidence. This gives them more personal influence and the stimulation of learning.

It recalibrates the basis of hierarchy and power; servant leaders use their formal power to empower others. In this sense, he is a journeyman along the road to mastery. For years, a good leader was the expert who knew the most or could do everything best. Servant-leadership is precisely not about wanting to lead and be imitated, but rather focuses on encouraging and guiding others' abilities.

A servant leader wants to make his employees completely independent, allow them as much control over their own work as possible and earn his total trust. If this evolution continues, it is possible that you yourself as a leader will become seemingly redundant or invisible.

After all, in the end, your employees will be able to do everything you expect. And then what?

From then on, it is less and less about 'where we want to go', and more and more about how to rise even further above ourselves (Collins, 2001). Indeed, once a leader is truly invisible or redundant, opportunities open up for which there was no time before. In the workplace, we can then become increasingly proactive and focus, for example, on innovation, networking and ongoing team development. There might be room for work expansion, for a new project, a new idea that can be built on.

However, there is also the possibility of taking on an (even greater) social responsibility as an organisation. How does our community benefit? Our country? Maybe even the world? Perhaps challenges that are 'greater' than the original objectives. Who doesn't want a climate-neutral company, for instance? Or who doesn't want to strive for a strong social fabric inside, as well as outside, their organisation? Servant leaders can always strive to increase their influence, always working to improve. In this way, they constantly try to focus on improving themselves and those around them. Because, as Eleanor Roosevelt succinctly put it, 'A good leader inspires people to have confidence in the leader, a great leader inspires people to have confidence in themselves.'

RECOMMENDATIONS ON THE FIVE CHARACTERISTICS OF A SERVANT LEADER

- Distinguish what you can influence and what you cannot influence. Be forward-looking. Focus on where you as a leader can make the biggest difference to the whole.

- Experiment with the method of the hand. That way, you will get to know your employees' operation manual. This will help create an atmosphere of psychological safety and trust.

- Be curious about what is going on with your employee, what drives him. Draw up core quadrants to get to know your employee better, to find the rationales behind his resistance and to handle conflict situations.

- Stay yourself, be authentic. Be transparent and have integrity.

- Focus on the growth of your employees. Always strive to increase their independence and responsibility. Dare to become invisible to increase your influence, both in the workplace and in the world.

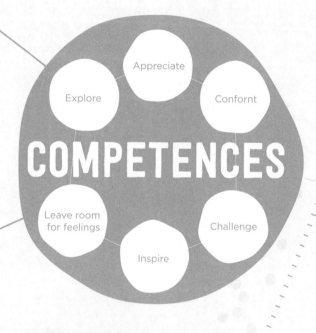

COMPETENCES

Appreciate

Explore

Confornt

Leave room
for feelings

Inspire

Challenge

SIX COMPETENCES
OF A **COACH**

SIX COMPETENCES OF A COACH

'The grass is greener where you water it'

— Neil Barringham

In this chapter, I zoom in on the manager's coaching role. The manager's approach to coaching could sometimes be confused with 'weak' leadership. This confusion arises when the manager does not dare to step into his leadership or guiding role, when he sets too few boundaries or does not sufficiently define his expectations. The servant leader is clear about his vision, yardstick and criteria (see Chapters 1 and 2). He also realises that the key to achieving a collectively supported and robust result lies in providing any necessary coaching support, ensuring that his employees can work independently and efficiently and feel competent.

However, while the guiding functions of leadership and monitoring professional standards are enforceable, coaching is not. Which is why I recommend that you 'announce' to your employees when you step into your role as coach (Clement, 2008). This can be done spontaneously and playfully:

'Shall we have a look at this together?'
'Do you mind if we talk about it for a while?'
'I could give you this or that advice, but shall we sit down for a moment?'

A coaching intervention is usually needed when complex situations arise. In such cases, it helps if a conversation proceeds in a structured manner. Every conversation you have as a coach can be built on the same pattern.

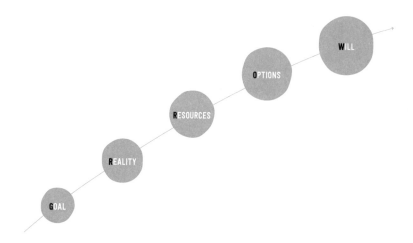

The GRROW model presented here encourages employees to think for themselves, which often proves very effective. After all, when an employee has thought of a solution or approach himself, he will usually be able to implement it well and with gusto.

'Chief, how could I organise my meetings more efficiently?
Everyone just sits there unprepared and they often don't respond when
I ask something.'

The GRROW model consists of five phases that can take place in a conversation. GRROW is an abbreviation for: Goal - Reality - Resources - Options - Will (Whitmore, 2010). These phases do not necessarily occur in this order. Often, a conversation starts with reality.

Goal
Find out the things the conversation should concretely deliver:

• Specifically, what should meetings look like?

• What do your colleagues do differently?

• Do you have examples of what they do differently?

- What should be the result of the meetings?
- How would that make you feel?

Or more generally:
- What do you want to achieve?
- What would the situation be like for you to be 'satisfied'?
- In what areas would you like to see change?
- What would you like to tackle?
- Where would you like to be after this conversation?
- How will you know the problem has been solved?

Reality

Explore the current situation with as open a mind as possible. Your function as coach now is to encourage your employee to self-analyse, in addition to analysing concrete examples. It is important to maintain the common thread and close off irrelevant tangents before they get very far. Concentrate on solving an existing problem. So don't go rooting around too much in 'how you got here', but together place the ladder on which your employee can climb out of the pit. Be aware that silence in a conversation can indicate that your employee's thinking process has been activated. So feel free to allow this. Sample questions could be:

- How exactly do you run the meetings?
- What is the effect of that?
- Where do they get stuck, do you think?
- What would you like to see, experience, hear more of at the meetings?
- Who or what else is at play?

Resources

What are tools or resources we can use? These can be in the person themselves, found in the environment or with others.

- When do meetings run smoothly? What happens then?
- What skills, qualities or resources do you already have that could be useful?
- What do you need?
- What could help you?
- Who is skilled in doing this; where could you learn this?
- Where can you find the necessary information?

Options

This is a creative phase in which you and your employee seek the best way to achieve the goal together. The trick here is to initiate a creative thought process and - not hindered by self-censorship or questions of feasibility - brainstorm freely. The more options formulated at this stage, the better. This ensures broad employee support. You should preferably let your employee do the talking in this phase; you promote the creative thinking process, provide structure in the output and only contribute ideas yourself if necessary. Sample questions during this phase could be:

- What alternatives do you have? Make a list of possible actions.
- What are the pros and cons of the different options?
- How could you try them out?

Will

All possible routes are now mapped out: which option will your employee choose? What does he want to throw his weight behind?

- Which option would give you the most satisfaction?
- Which approach appeals to you?
- What is the simplest first step?
- How could you address this in a different way?

Finally, you make a clear action plan together on what the employee will undertake:

- What is the first thing you do and when?
- What do you think is the most promising possibility?
- Are there any obstacles? What can you do to resolve them?

In this introduction, we have mainly looked at the content of the conversation: what is someone's goal and how does he achieve it? The servant leader is an inspiring coach who creates a learning climate that makes it attractive to come up with innovative ideas. We can also look at conversations from the manager himself: what skills can he use as a coach to help achieve an optimal result?

I cover six of them: explore, appreciate, engage, confront, challenge, inspire and leave room for feelings. First, we'll go through them in a nutshell.

When an employee brings up a situation, the coach first of all tries to explore. After all, he is curious and wants to get a picture of the situation, the obstacle, the goal or desire of the employee. The coach will be mindful to express his appreciation. He will not only look at the results or performance, but also at small steps in the employee's development: an original idea, expressing his dissatisfaction or questioning his own conviction. When employees receive appreciation, they often feel a greater need for correction and adjustment. Employees may then come and ask the manager to let them know if they can do something better or differently.

Through this appreciation, the manager creates a climate in which engaged confrontation can thrive. Now and then, confrontation is perceived as a gift. However, confronting an employee - even if there is deep down appreciation - will usually turn into resistance. Appreciation and confrontation are two sides of the same coin: giving feedback. Employees come to a coach to experience a difference. Stretching the person is called challenging, stretching the content is called inspiring. By challenging the employee, you express your confidence in his ability. When we inspire, we add something to the content: we broaden someone's perspective or offer them a new way of seeing. During a coaching intervention, however, all kinds of emotions soon come into play. Giving space to these feelings ensures, among other things, that the challenges remain manageable and achievable for the employee.

A TOOL FOR YOUR TEAM

Practice shows that adding some visual flair to the GRROW conversation makes things run more smoothly. Here, we combine the GRROW method with the four phases of "speaking out, discussing, agreeing and addressing." In our coaching conversations, we look for the deeper layers, but before we get there, we allow ourselves time to slow down for a moment. In this way, we create a relaxed atmosphere of "de-meeting."

We are curious and really want to understand what is going on. Therefore, we take the time to let the person you are coaching talk through the issue at length and in detail. Often, the core theme unfolds by itself. Only when we have grasped that, do we step up a gear in the conversation. We then discuss all possible options and ultimately come to a clear and unequivocal agreement.

Enjoy a stimulating dip in the current of your GRROW conversation.

COLLABORATIVE CONVERSATIONS

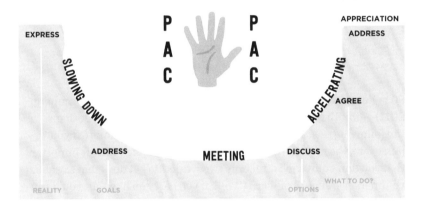

1. EXPLORE

'True knowledge consists in knowing that one knows nothing.'

— Socrates'

On a sweltering summer evening, you sit at the table next to your cousin Jackson, who is studying business administration. You ask how he is doing. He says that after two weeks he has had quite enough of his holiday job. He was promised exciting, instructive work. In the course of the conversation, Jackson becomes increasingly emotional: 'Now all I do is make copies, distribute papers and other administrative jobs. That is not at all what they promised. I'm really sick of it. You know what? On Monday I'll go to my boss and he'll see!'

90 per cent of people presented with the case study above (Rosenberg, 2011) admit they do not (yet) really hear what's being said. Perhaps the following reactions are recognisable: offering solutions ('If you persevere, the job will probably change'), moralising ('Isn't it important that you don't quit a job after only two weeks? What does that say about your perseverance?') or warn ('Well, if you carry on like this, you'll run out of money. That doesn't seem like a good idea either, does it?'). But what is your cousin actually saying in essence? If you listen to his story, you hear that he is disappointed. It is only when this emotion is heard that there is room for exchange and bonding can occur.

The importance of showing your interest as a coach can hardly be overestimated. Look at curiosity as the engine that powers the coach. It's essential to try to imagine what the employee is struggling with or what exactly he wants.

For a coach, offering unsolicited advice is often tempting. Someone comes to you with a problem and you want to solve it immediately. However, this approach has risks:

- The solution is ridiculous. Your solution isn't an answer to the actual problem.

- The employee doesn't make the solution his own; he implements it haphazardly.

- The employee isn't forced to think for himself.

- .The employee becomes convinced that he can't think of solutions himself, but has to come to you.

- The employee doesn't increase his self-management skills. He may start coming to you for every little problem.

- The employee holds you accountable if your solution doesn't turn out well.

To be clear: I don't think there's anything wrong with a coach helping to consider and brainstorm about solutions. In my view, the main thing is getting the employee's perspective fully on the table before thinking about options and solutions in any meaningful way. The basic attitude of the servant coach is to be Curious, Open, and Truthful when engaging with employees. This helps you focus and really listen to the other person. By showing your interest and curiosity, you'll achieve a more meaningful conversation.

You discover what the actual question is, while hearing about stumbling blocks or blockages. You search for the 'question behind the question':

- Tell us: what exactly is the process like?

- What happened during the meeting?

- What could help you, do you think?

One of the great challenges in coaching is to make abstract concepts concrete (Clement, 2008). After all, if things remain abstract, we seem to agree quickly. Everyone probably wants more 'open communication and respect' in their team. Of course you expect 'employee commitment'. But what exactly do these terms mean? What are the concrete expectations of the employee and the manager? Indeed, what one person means by commitment, open communication or respect may be something fundamentally different from what another does. It is therefore important to translate such terms into tangible, nameable facts. If the coach is curious and really tries to picture the employee's question, desire or situation, abstract terms often translate into examples and concrete descriptions:

- Give an example.

- What exactly do you mean by that?

- How can I visualise that?

- Describe - as concretely as in a movie scene - when you would be satisfied with a solution?

Open and unbiased listening to your employee's situational picture sometimes works, sometimes not. In this regard, be honest and transparent. Besides listening to the employee, also listen to yourself. Your opinion about the situation, for example, may hinder your ability to engage in dialogue. Or sometimes you are preoccupied with your own worries or with what you want to do when this conversation ends. We could see these reactions as obstacles to communication, but then it sounds like they would be 'bad'. My message is not that these reactions should not exist. On the contrary. These reflexes make it clear that you don't quite have the mental space yet to really listen to what the other person is trying to convey. That you need to listen to yourself first. The trick will be to communicate about it transparently, allowing you to really give space to the other person. You can do this by dual messaging (Clement, 2008), which creates space for both yourself and the employee to really listen:

- You do not yet have a handle on the issue raised by the employee ('I would like to help, but I still don't see where you are stuck.').

- You think your co-worker is wrong ('I think differently myself and I am curious to know how you see it. Convince me I'm wrong.').

- You don't have time. State this honestly and schedule a new appointment ('I don't have time right now, but I really do want to hear your story. Give me a call this afternoon?').

- You have your own solution ('I would solve it like that. What do you think?').

EXPLORING IN PRACTICE

A useful tool to help you picture the employee's situation or goal as vividly as possible is the LSQ method: Listening - Summarizing - Questioning. Listen to your employee, summarize his message and then ask questions.

Listen
When you are curious about what is going on with the other person, why they react this way or that way or have a certain belief, you no longer allow yourself to be guided by presuppositions or your personal opinion about the person, but listen to the information they give you.

Summarize
To summarize means to boil down in your own words the most important things the other person has said. A summary sends the essence of the message, as you understood it. You may summarize the content of a message. Or sometimes you notice that someone seems very cheerful, enthusiastic or anxious in their story. Then you can also return the feeling they seem to be experiencing.

The purpose of asking questions is to help the other person put their thoughts into words and clarify the problem. There is a distinction between open questions and closed questions. The choice depends on the goal you want to achieve. With an open-ended question, you broaden the conversation:

- What happened?
- How did that conversation go?
- What's stopping you from doing that?
- What makes you say that?
- What exactly do you mean by that?

With a closed question, you bring clarity and focus to the conversation. You can direct the conversation or briefly check whether you've understood the other person correctly, for example:

- So there is ... going on?
- Are there any witnesses?
- Are you the person responsible for ...?

EXERCISE

For a few moments a day, try just listening to the other person. If your mind is not free, you can experiment with dual messaging. Summarise what you hear and ask only probing questions. Be curious and use your imagination.

2. APPRECIATE

In general, Jill (aged 17) is not a great student, but she is an absolute whiz at maths. Proving theorems, calculating integrals and analysing statistics she experiences as playing rather than working. She achieved a whopping 92 per cent in her exams. For everything else, however, her marks were all just above 50 per cent, and for French, she only received 44 per cent. She tells you despondently that her parents had been very angry about that failing grade.

Research by Boyatzis (2006) shows that over 50 per cent of interventions by others who want to help us start by stressing our 'weaknesses'. People are quick to put forward any blind spots or difficulties to explain a situation. This sometimes works, but by no means always. Just think about which subjects you liked the least in secondary school ... Perhaps you didn't really care about developing your skills in these subjects.

80 per cent of the interventions by others that actually changed us started with an affirmation of our strengths (Boyatzis, 2006). Of course, in practice, you engage with both weaknesses and strengths. But the greatest margin for growth often lies where there is already an aptitude.

Jill has already discovered her passion and her talent! Seeing and appreciating this means that Jill could study civil engineering next year. Being able to do that will give her the motivation to work hard and make up for her failing French in the next semester, so she is not kept back from doing what she excels at.

Emphasising what works well is an important lever to get or keep employees moving ahead. Where the employee has a talent is where the development area, the area for growth, is greatest. Paying attention to

this as a coach can help maximise the employee's potential.
In concrete terms, this means that we try to reinforce and empower every improvement and progress we see by showing our appreciation. To be clear, we're not just talking about appreciating performance. The road to results is littered with opportunities to praise an employee's steps along the way and their attempts to improve: the employee has a good idea, expresses disagreement with you or has an original angle. This may seem obvious, yet I notice that managers are sometimes sparing with their compliments. They understand the importance of showing appreciation, but at the same time do not always offer it generously. When it comes to dealing with appreciation, we may not always feel comfortable. There could be several reasons why:

- How will the other person react if I compliment him?

- Suppose he thinks I don't really mean it?

- Suppose he doesn't believe it's deserved or thinks I have ulterior motives?

- When I get a compliment, I often find it hard to receive. Maybe he feels the same way?

- Once I start, should I keep giving compliments?

- Suppose the other person starts resting on his laurels when I say he is doing well?

Such reflections may make you uncomfortable about showing appreciation. As a result, you do it less spontaneously or not at all. If you run into this sometimes, you can conveniently resolve this by dual messaging, just as you do when exploring to discover the crux of an issue (Clement, 2008). Show both your concern and appreciation for the employee. Share your inner reflections with the other person:

- 'I feel a bit uncomfortable saying this, but I appreciate that you so often step in for your colleagues.'

- Maybe you think it's normal to 'just do your job', but I really appreciate your efforts.'

- 'Even though we are only sitting together for the first time ..., I appreciate your honesty about the lack of support you've had your first few days as a newcomer.'

So a coach is vigilant about complimenting. Not only because he knows it makes sense and works, but also because he looks at his employee with an appreciative eye. He is aware that the image he has (developed) of his employee permeates everything he says or doesn't say, asks or doesn't ask, does or doesn't do.

APPRECIATING EMPLOYEES IN PRACTICE

This argument for appreciation notwithstanding, your compliment won't work if the employee doesn't feel like you mean it. Employees mainly sense what you feel about them by the way you look at them rather than what you say. Don't praise someone if you do not mean it. You create an appreciative climate mainly by looking at people appreciatively. It goes beyond a compliment or a pat on the back. It is an attitude. This creates a climate of trust, transparency and encouragement. The employee will find his rhythm more easily and be willing to give his best. This can bring about the need for adjustment and correction. The employee feels confirmed and wants to know what can be done better. Appreciation is a foundation for a comfortable learning climate. As in many other cases, strive to make your compliments concrete. Statements, depending on the context, can have their value ('I'm glad you're on my team', 'You're a flexible colleague'), but because they are general and vague, they are often harder to give as well as to receive. It's better to keep your compliments limited and specific:

'Just now when the meeting fell silent, you took the initiative to draw a plan on the flipchart and that gave the meeting a boost. I appreciate that.' 'I saw how you calmly and patiently explained the new mail programme to your colleague. I like seeing you being so helpful.'

EXERCISE

Think about the past week. What statement or behaviour did you praise? Keep it to small and specific acts.

3. CONFRONT

'Sometimes it takes tough love to avoid false kindness'

— Anonymous

What do you do when your partner walks into the kitchen in muddy boots? You don't hesitate to say something about it, right? And when your daughter shows you a picture she drew, don't you give 'feedback' immediately? Or do you wait until the annual meeting? Why do you manage to do at home something that is more difficult at work?

> *A while ago, I was involved in training a team of speech therapists. I asked the group for feedback. One of the participants said, "In the last three minutes, you've said 'eh' 11 times and that distracts me as a speech therapist.*

Only once in five years did I receive this kind of feedback. You often hear talk of positive and negative feedback. The above example could fall under negative feedback. But you could also approach it differently. For instance, this group was the first to draw my attention to the fact that I should pay attention to over-using a filler word, even though many people before them had probably thought the same thing. Having this feedback gives me the opportunity to act on it or not. After all, if no one had told me, I would never have known about it.

Confronting and showing appreciation are essentially the same thing: giving something back to someone in an honest way. Here, you can say something about someone's beliefs, their behaviour, their opinion or how you feel about them. There is nothing inherently negative about correction and nothing positive about appreciation. It is just feedback on how something affects what you think (or don't think), what you say (or don't say), what you do (or don't do) in a given situation. Feedback is just feedback.

Because we sometimes find getting along with an employee difficult, it is interesting to explore where the difficulty comes from. It is often easier to keep your criticism to yourself. The fear of hurting someone, of giving someone the idea that they are not doing a good job or causing damage to the relationship, can lead us not to voice our comments.

Actually, you are depriving someone of an opportunity. You could say that the other person has the right to know what is going on inside you, because only then does he have the opportunity to do something with your information. You give him a gift, so to speak, by partially breaking the guardedness between you. You indicate that you feel the relationship is strong enough to be transparent in what you think.

So although a confrontation can be a gift, it will rarely be received that way, especially if the employee does not experience curiosity or appreciation. In that case, even if he feels you have a good point, he will resist. This 'recalcitrance' is a logical reaction: the employee feels reduced to a fault, so to speak, because he does not feel truly seen or heard for who he is. People want – even more than being proved right - to be heard. If there is a solid foundation of curiosity and appreciation in the relationship, there is more chance that the correction or adjustment will be seen as a gift.

> *Rita keeps leaving her dirty coffee cup on the counter and not in the dishwasher. When you notice this the first time, you let it slide. But then you start noticing it several times a day. If you don't communicate to her about this, you start communicating with yourself. In your inner dialogue, your image of Rita gradually changes. It is then no longer Rita-who-doesn't-put-her-cup-in-the-dishwasher, but Rita-the-careless. You then have to vent about her to colleagues. But you can't do that! From that reinforced image, you approach the next situation involving Rita. The risk is obvious. Escalation is coming.*

Anything unsaid seeks its way into the light. Whether that is within yourself (inner dialogue: 'She is so careless!'), or addressing the person in question (asking suggestive questions: 'Hey Rite, have you noticed we have a dishwasher?'), with colleagues (gossiping: 'That's someone who just doesn't care about others!') or at home (in private: 'You'll never believe what I've had to put up with today!'). An image of Rita is reinforced and before you know it, it takes on a life of its own. The person's behaviour is influencing you. Therefore, quickly react and let someone know how their actions effect you; after all, it is an investment in the relationship. Otherwise, you will be tempted to make statements about someone's character ('Rita is careless') and there will be no limit to what might happen next.

SYMPATHETIC CONFRONTATION IN PRACTICE

When you swallow your criticism, you often find yourself harbouring two messages in your head: the content of what you want to say and the concern you have for the relationship (Clement, 2008). So obviously, it is difficult to give feedback if you don't add a relationship message. You stumble because you are only mentioning half of what is actually going on in your head. After all, you want the relationship to stay good as well as being able to confront someone with your criticism. A method to connect the two is giving a relational message, in addition to the substantive one.

Jeffrey has been promoted to team leader. He manages his former colleagues, including his friend Tom. Tom has already been late three times this week and other colleagues have to step up each time as a result. Jeffrey wants to set limits in regards to being late (content), but finds it difficult because he doesn't want Tom to think he is arrogant because of his new position (care). Jeffrey: 'I wouldn't want you to think now that I'm 'acting so different' or suddenly feeling superior. Still, for the sake of peaceful cooperation, I have to tell you something. This week, you came late three times without telling anyone why. This forced the other guys to work longer and kept them in the dark as to why you were late.'

Other examples of relationship messages:

- 'I wouldn't want our cooperation to suffer.'
- 'I don't want to hurt you.'
- 'I really should have told you this a long time ago.'
- 'I don't want to take away your enthusiasm.'

Note: a relationship message is different from expressing appreciation. If you introduce your criticism with a compliment, you will both hollow out your compliment and invalidate the criticism you are about to deliver. Also, avoid putting suggestions in your questions. ('Could you have made so many errors in the meeting report because you wrote it too quickly?', 'Do you think your fatigue could have something to do with your eating habits?'). Then you quickly run the risk of coming across as manipulative and fake.

Either way, it is often inevitable that your employee will take the criticism personally. The trick is to play the ball and not the man. Your feedback is about someone's actions, the way they approach something, their beliefs or how they look at certain things. To be as accurate as possible, it can help to keep in mind exactly what you are finding fault with. You then describe as factually or as specifically as possible what you are criticising and possibly what the effect is. Experience the difference between the following statements:

- 'You are so careless sometimes, now those files are out of order again.'

  or:

- 'Among the files you brought in yesterday, there were three forms on budget formatting that were missing (description of facts), leaving the board with questions (impact).'

- 'The topics at the meeting this morning did not captivate you?'

  or:

- 'I didn't hear you at the meeting this morning (description of someone's actions). I wonder if everything is okay with you (effect).'

- 'You really are a control freak anyway.'

  or:

- 'If you see it as your job to control all tasks in detail (description of someone's beliefs), it seems logical to me that your employees will not feel responsible for it (effect).'

A TOOL FOR YOUR TEAM

We developed a tool for confronting someone in an engaging way:

EXERCISE

Imagine you need to convey a difficult message to one of your employees. Then go through the four steps of this method and practise presenting your message in front of the mirror.

SYMPATHETIC CONFRONTATION

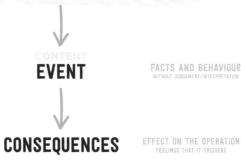

RELATIONSHIP MESSAGE

WHAT IS YOUR INTENTION IN DELIVERING THIS MESSAGE?
WHY DO IT?

WHAT MAKES YOU (DARE) NOT GIVE THE MESSAGE?
WHY NOT?

CONTENT

EVENT   FACTS AND BEHAVIOUR
WITHOUT JUDGEMENT/INTERPRETATION

CONSEQUENCES   EFFECT ON THE OPERATION
FEELINGS THAT IT TRIGGERS

FROM NOW ON:

SPEAK OUT: Keep a silence, check if your colleague understands what you
are saying.
Leave room for emotion. Be an OEN.

TALK IT OVER: : Look for the essential reason why we keep running into this
problem.
Use LSQ. Focus on the Goal: How do we work this out
together?

DISCUSS: Look for options and solutions that can really make a
difference

AGREE: Who does what by when?
Be SMART.

4. CHALLENGE

'Faith is to believe what you do not see; the reward of this faith is to see what you believe.'

— Saint Augustine

As a coach, you not only support, you also challenge the other person to go further than they would on their own. By challenge, I mean that you encourage someone to push their limits and tap into their enthusiasm, while supporting them in doing so. A challenging coach will stimulate his employee to go one step further. He will support his employees, enabling them to gain self-confidence, take care of themselves develop their talents and take on more responsibility. A coach will help look for any possible personal challenges his employees face.
Some examples:

- Support someone who is drowning in work to not start a new project right away, but to set their own priorities first.

- Challenging someone to make choices that mean more to themselves.

- Helping someone make a difficult conversation go well anyway.

Challenging is a logical extension of appreciation. What your employee has a talent for and is 'naturally' good at, also requires further development. When we know the talents of our employees, we can empower and use them in the team. Be alert to signs of strengths in the employee, to what is already going well. He can often use these strengths elsewhere. If you make his successes explicit, dynamics are created and the learning process switches up a gear. The other person feels empowered in what he can do and is challenged.

Challenging - stimulating someone to push beyond his former limits and supporting him in doing so - is a way for a coach to demonstrate his confidence in someone's potential. Not just with words, but by proving that you believe in him. What happens between the lines is that the manager has expressed confidence in his employee. This is a step beyond showing appreciation.

When you actively challenge people, you push them out of their comfort zone. A child's first step also occurs because the former balance is momentarily disturbed. So learning can be exciting. Comfort or balance will briefly give way to (learning) tension. Understandably, an employee is not necessarily always eager for a challenge that will take him out of his comfort zone. An initial reaction may be uncertainty, doubt or even fear. When employees are challenged to try something new, for example, it often causes stress ('Will that work?', 'Will I be able to handle that?', 'Is that really for me?'). This is what happens on the surface. Don't immediately 'believe' your employee when he reacts reluctantly ('I can't see myself doing that', 'It's beyond me'). As a coach, be especially curious about the concern, fear or need behind this reluctance. Give space to his feelings and reservations. I discuss why this is so important in the last section of this chapter.

For an employee, on the other hand, being challenged can be very important. Suppose he sees you challenging his colleague, chances are he will wonder why you don't ask him to do the same ('I'm capable of that too, aren't I?'). In that respect, I believe every employee wants to be challenged in his or her own way. Sometimes it is just a matter for the employee to encounter that coach who - finally - sees his potential. He may not necessarily remember what was said in an intervention, but perhaps how the coach looked at him or how much he believed in him.

EXERCISE

Have a conversation with an employee. Review the past year together and ask the following questions (Clement, 2008): think back to a specific moment when you felt you were doing well, when you felt you were on fire. Describe your experience: what happened?
What did you do? Who was there? What did others do? What was the effect on yourself and others? Name in detail what made the experience so rewarding and what your part was. Based on these answers, move on to the next question: what would you like to see more of in the coming day (week, month, year)?

CHALLENGING IN PRACTICE

As coach, after exploring to discover what the employee wants, you can ask the question directly. When will he truly be satisfied? When will a real difference be made?

It is certainly not always about having to do more, faster or better. It is also certainly not about turning every problem into a 'challenge'. Instead, think of a challenge as a gift that you give at an opportune time. And just like giving a gift, it is important that it is adapted to the person and that the timing is right.

Some examples of concrete challenges:

• Learning to say 'no' while making sure the relationship stays good. Or even improves it.

• Assisting less, yet still being perceived as more supportive by your employees.

• Starting a difficult conversation with an employee and taking the relationship to a higher level as a result.

Some examples of challenging interventions:

- Let yourself go: what would you really like?
- What will it take for you to get excited about this idea?

You can also go a bit further than merely challenging and provoking. For instance, you go all in on the other person's problem, you admit that indeed nothing will help, you dramatize or trivialize the problem completely. This approach works especially well if it starts from your authentic commitment (and usually this is accompanied by a touch of humour). As a coach, you should only do this type of intervention after you have assessed whether your relationship with your employee can handle it. Sometimes you can surprise someone so much through provocation that the situation thaws, that space opens up. Because someone is caught completely off guard, the conversation may short-circuit for a while.

- I'll give some examples of provocative coaching statements:
- Exaggerating: 'I think this situation is deadlocked.'
- Dramatizing: 'I've never seen it so bad!'
- Throwing oil on the fire: 'This is completely hopeless!'
- Acquiescing: 'I think you are completely right.'
- Going along with someone's 'victim position': 'This situation, in my opinion, will never improve.'
- Going along with someone's judgement: 'It's true, he's a total slacker.'

While making such a remark, look at your employee with an empowering and challenging gaze. What extra resources does he have within him than he is currently using? What does he have a talent for? Where does his challenge lie? What would happen if he took more risks?

5. INSPIRE

*'What people fear is not the darkness that surrounds them,
but the light that shines within them.'*

— Nelson Mandela

*Imagine going to sleep tonight and a miracle happens: all the worries
you had from your work suddenly disappear as the sun rises. You
breathe in the fresh morning air and feel that a burden has fallen off
your shoulders (adapted freely from Insoo Kim Berg).*

In our culture, we often analyse and dissect problems or challenges
and then tackle them step by step. We often obtain excellent results in
doing things this way. However, a possible disadvantage is that we never
think out of the box. That we never once just try something completely
different. While inspiring others, we might turn our approach
completely around. We pretend for a moment that the problem or
obstacle does not exist. What would the future look like then?

Inspire comes from the Latin word inspirare, to inhale or breathe in.
We also recognise the word spiritus, which we translate as spirit or soul.
So an inspirational coach is someone who has the ability to 'in-spirit' -
inspire, and animate others.

Sometimes we encounter a recurring limitation or resistance. But a
situation is never completely deadlocked. A problem never occurs
constantly or all week. The seeds of change are usually already hidden
within the current problem. Translated to our work situations in
teams, we will look at a problem for those seeds, which are often still
exceptional at that moment. Looking at a situation appreciatively is not
purely about looking for positives just because we want to compliment.
It is a way of critically analysing reality, with a special eye on what

works, where there is growth potential or room for development. If you want to empower what works, you can look for exceptions:

- Where did the problem trouble us the least?
- Where did we succeed in spite of it? How did that happen?
- What works, and what could you do more of?
- What do others say works?
- When will it get better?
- When is the best time to deal with it?
- When is the problem less present?

EXERCISE

Person A asks person B the questions below, first working through the first round of questions and then the second.

What is your problem?	What would be a good outcome of this conversation?
Hoelang heb je er al last van?	
How long has it been bothering you?	Suppose your problem is solved, what then will be different?
Why do you think you have this problem?	What have you done so far that worked, even if it only helped a little?
Why do you think it is a difficult problem?	How have you solved similar problems in the past?
What do you see as the causes of your problem?	What will work best?
What is keeping you from finding a solution?	What else could you do?
Who or what could help?	What will you do next?

Discuss together the difference between the effect of the questions in rounds 1 and 2:

- What is the difference for A while asking the questions?
- What is the difference for B in answering the questions?

To inspire, we try to get employees to think from a hypothetical, ideal situation. For this, you can use different angles.

INSPIRING IN PRACTICE

Specifically, you can inspire in three different ways. Depending on the situation and the employee, as a coach you can assess which way is most appropriate.

Inspirational reframing

As a coach, you can invite your employee to look at the same situation with new glasses. The basic idea here is that a 'problem' does not exist in itself, but only becomes one by looking at it in a certain way. You are playing with changing points of view, so to speak. So is one more 'true' than the other? No. But probably no less either.

Examples of re-framing:

'We have an open conflict after an accumulation of irritations' (problem)

or:

'This is a great opportunity to get to know each other's needs and improve cooperation sustainably.' (reframing)
'Feedback is threatening and awkward' (problem)

or:

'Someone around you is taking the trouble of giving you feedback about the effects of your actions. Now you have a chance to learn something from that.' (reframing)

Other examples of re-framing:

- How would you look at this in a year's time?

- Imagine you were your own grandfather. What would you say to yourself on this topic?

- What do you think this would be like for the customer?

- Suppose you could give yourself advice right now, what would you advise yourself to do?

- How would colleague x handle this?

Inspiring innovation

It is not natural for everyone to try a new solution. Looking for creative solutions therefore often means dealing with inexperience, uncertainty and sometimes even fear.

As with brainstorming, temporarily suspending your judgement is an essential feature of a creative approach. Indeed, often emerging ideas are dismissed too quickly ('This is not feasible', 'What will people think of this?'). Rash judgment can hinder the development of a good idea. The trick is to throw unusual ideas on the table and look at them together in a relaxed way. Only when there are enough ideas on the table can we judge their quality. What would be the effects? What might work, what might not? Perhaps several ideas can be combined into a solution.

Sample questions:

- What are the non-obvious options?

- What is the craziest idea you can think of in this regard?

- Imagine for a moment that you wouldn't have to justify your idea, that no one would ever see it but yourself. What would you do then?

- What is the common denominator between the ideas? Can we connect them into one idea?

Inspiring advice

As a coach, it sometimes happens that you think of a possible solution yourself during a conversation. If we see coaching as provoking and supporting learning, in my view it would be a waste not to bring your advice into the conversation. The only question is how to make it part of the thought process and not provide a ready-made solution that the employees implement without making it their own. At times when an idea bubbles up in your head, you can tell your employees. The trick will be to check whether it was helpful for them to be handed an idea at that moment.

Sample questions:

- Can you do something with this idea?
  What would be your variation on this idea?

- Which of the three solutions do you personally think is the best?

- Why might that idea be a solution to your particular problem?

- Can you list the pros and cons for your situation?

- Based on this, can you create a variant that is more suitable for you?

6. LEAVE ROOM FOR FEELINGS

'Reculer pour mieux sauter.' (fall back to better advance)

— French proverb

TDuring a coaching session, you will often see your employee become enthusiastic, beaming with pride; you may detect their self-confidence increasing. It may also be that there are feelings getting in the way that seem to prevent what we want to achieve: fear, insecurity, doubt, resistance, indifference or even anger. For most people, bringing up these feelings is slightly uncomfortable, or they don't immediately feel comfortable with them. As a result, we then start fighting them, consciously or unconsciously.

> Samantha is an HR officer in a petrochemical company. She has spent the last two weeks doing market research on a new HR software system. She is asked to give a presentation to the management team. She relates her nervousness to her supervisor.

A possible response from the manager could be: 'Oh well, you shouldn't be afraid of that, they don't bite!' However, by doing so, the manager denies the reason for the existence of Samantha's feelings, which does her no good. A better reaction might be: 'You find it exciting, don't you? I can understand that ...'

When feelings are denied or contradicted, they strengthen. They seek another channel. Feelings always find a way. Unconsciously, they start to influence someone's behaviour: an employee bottles up his emotions, or he compensates for his feelings (fear becomes frustration, for instance). You might not really help someone who feels insecure by saying 'there is no reason to feel uncertain about it' or 'it will all work out'. Someone who challenges a decision has no use for someone advising him to 'not let them bully you' or 'just learn to deal with change'. The trick for a coach is to allow and welcome these feelings.

By giving space to 'troublesome' feelings that seem to get in our way, they can serve as a bridge to enthusiasm. When we skilfully handle these 'bothersome' feelings, we are listening to what they are trying to tell us. In our minds, we distinguish between 'good' and 'bad' feelings. Pride, confidence and joy belong to the first category; fear, anger and disappointment to the second. But isn't it a fallacy to classify these feelings into 'positive' and 'negative'? In themselves, there is nothing positive about the first set, nothing negative about the second. What is true is that we are more comfortable with the first set and less comfortable with the second.

However, you could also see them as the front and back of the same basic feeling. Then the connection between these 'positive' and 'negative' feelings stands out. Behind fear is a need for safety or daring, doubt points to the need for certainty or clarity. Indifference tells us that there is not yet enough reason to feel commitment; anger refers to indignation, or a conflict with something we consider important. All these are things you can explore in practice.

GIVING SPACE IN PRACTICE

Above all, emotions want to be felt and experienced. Experience teaches us that emotions that are given a chance to be felt may take up more space initially, only to clear a path for something new. When, as a manager, you do not dismiss, relativize, gloss over or counteract feelings or doubts, you give your employee space to feel them, so that they dissipate naturally.

The employee experiences that it is okay to be anxious and have doubts. This makes room for a new perspective or new enthusiasm. As a coach, we realize emotions are telling us something. Just as they can block actions, the coach can sometimes use them to remove obstacles. I zoom in on two feelings: fear/uncertainty and resistance (Clement, 2008).

Fear/uncertainty

When someone is anxious or insecure, the right thing is to let these feelings exist. Our tendency to reassure someone, to say it will be all right, tells us that we find fear an awkward feeling. Out of concern for ourselves or the other person, we then quickly want to get rid of it. This fear of fear rarely has the effect of making the fear disappear.

What can fear tell us? Fear or insecurity indicates anxiety (to want to do something very well, to avoid failure, to not be rejected, etc.). With this, fear indicates high commitment and concern for oneself, others or the environment. When we start exploring fear, it can be felt, given space and relaxed. Often the employee's anxiety has its origins in all kinds of 'having to do this or that'. For example, someone 'has to give' an excellent presentation. It could be argued that when the 'has to' becomes too much, the 'want' is forgotten. When we descend into fear or uncertainty, we can explore together what the employee actually wants. From those desires come chances for initiative and boldness.

Resistance

The top executives of an organisation decide to introduce performance appraisals. They ask their managers to sit down once a year for an hour with each of their employees to talk about their cooperation, the employee's well-being and development. The executives get backlash. They experience resistance. Managers are said to be reluctant to follow along and are stuck in old patterns. Maybe a training course on Dealing with Change will help?

In this example, it may be clear that both parties feel 'resistance'. Concerns about a lack of enthusiasm or a backlash indicates resistance. When we examine this resistance, however, we discover much more concrete feelings or concerns:

- Have we been deficient all along, then?

- I don't see the point of such a conversation yet.

- I wouldn't know how to start such a conversation.

- I don't see how these talks are going to add any value.

- Everything is running smoothly now, right?

These feelings or concerns can be explored and concretised. If the managers feel that the executives are curious about their resistance, then there will soon be more willingness to tackle the situation in a constructive way.

If you notice that certain feelings are taking over in different areas of life (e.g. fear of failure), we recommend that you do not dabble in them as a manager. As a coach, you act as a servant, but you remain the guardian of professional standards. If you fail to make agreements about the yardstick with the troubled employee, the effect may be that the employee loses face with his colleagues. If this isolates the colleague, no one will benefit.

I recommend engaging in conversation in a coach-like, neutral way. After active and genuinely interested listening, the focus is on the question: 'What can I do for you, that will give you both the space to deal with the difficult situation and ensure that we don't fall foul of the norm?' So we make the translation to the shop floor, out of concern for the employee (and the results).

As a manager, even in your role as a coach, you are never a counsellor. Moreover, you cannot provide the security of a consulting relationship because you are also an evaluator of the work. If you sense that your employee requires professional help, a proper referral is more appropriate. Through everything you say, do or express non-verbally, the employee will experience first-hand how you see him. An employee who does not yet believe in himself and comes to a coach who does, is faced with the challenge to look at himself differently. As a coach, focus on your employee as someone who will succeed, who will find his way even if he does not yet know how. Visualise, conjure up images in your mind of what your employee will succeed at.

You are not doing your employee a favour if you are unrealistic about his abilities. However, setting someone's limits together does not have to diminish your belief in your employee and his qualities. The main thing is not to underestimate your employees. You can create a relaxed learning climate by looking at your employee in an empowering way and breathing relaxedly. This often brings humour and fun into the conversation, and lightness and airiness. Later, statements like: 'My coach helped me regain my self-confidence' or 'Because of his belief in me, I dared to take the first step' can follow.

- Teach your employee to enjoy feedback. Appreciate and confront where you can. Break through caution.

- As a coach, try to make a difference. One way you can achieve this is by challenging the person. By doing that, you express your confidence in his ability.

- Expand someone's perspective or offer them a new way of seeing things. That way, you can inspire them.

- Leave room for feelings and ensure a relaxed learning environment.

IN CONCLUSION

In Part II, I elaborated on the three roles of manager, leader and coach. When we add these themes to the framework of Part I, a new framework emerges:

The leader	The organisation		ABC of the employees
THE MANAGER will ...	give **space** by insisting on results **guide** the flow of activities	use four styles: • instructing • directing or guiding • facilitating • delegating	→ **AUTONOMY** He wants to take responsibility and to a large extent, be able to decide for himself how to tackle something
THE LEADER will ...	give **direction**, and guard the vision strengthen **relationships**	use five • characteristics: • proactive • empathetic • authentic • curious • invisible	→ **BONDING WITH THE GOAL AND WITH THE TEAM** He wants to contribute to a meaningful goal in a good atmosphere.
DE COACH will ...	define **roles** by focusing on talent stimulate **reflection** in a safe learning climate	use six skills: • explore • appreciate • engage • confront • challenge • inspire • allow space	→ **COMPETENCE** He wants to be good at something and be appreciated for it.

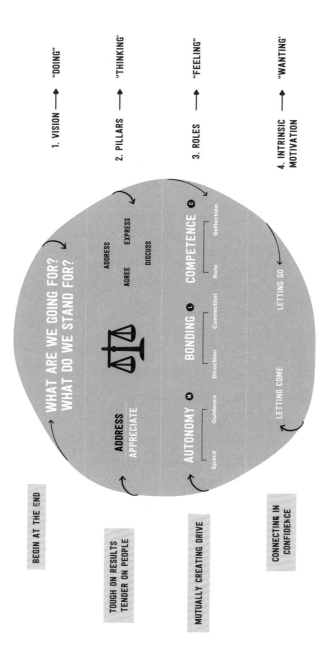

1. VISION → "DOING"

2. PILLARS → "THINKING"

3. ROLES → "FEELING"

4. INTRINSIC MOTIVATION → "WANTING"

WHAT ARE WE GOING FOR?
WHAT DO WE STAND FOR?

ADDRESS
APPRECIATE

ADDRESS
AGREE   EXPRESS
DISCUSS

AUTONOMY M   BONDING L   COMPETENCE C

Space   Guidance   Direction   Connection   Role   Reflection

LETTING COME   LETTING GO

BEGIN AT THE END

TOUGH ON RESULTS
TENDER ON PEOPLE

MUTUALLY CREATING DRIVE

CONNECTING IN
CONFIDENCE

A TOOL FOR YOUR TEAM

To measure your team's motivation, we have created a questionnaire called 'Our Team's Drive.' This questionnaire consists of 35 statements that highlight the motivation of each team member. You can easily rate the statements on a scale of 1 to 5 via the following link: www.servant-leadership.world. For each statement, you can indicate what you want to keep, what you want to see more of, or what you want to see less of. After filling in, you get a handy overview in PDF format!

When you let your team members fill in the questionnaire, you will get a clear picture of where you can make adjustments as a manager to boost your team's drive. Below is an overview of the 35 statements, grouped according to the themes in this book.

I. Bonding

A. Direction

1. My organisation's vision for delivering service is clear.
2. I stand by the vision of my organisation.
3. The organisational vision has been reiterated concretely enough in our team to use as a compass in my daily actions.
4. On a daily basis, I feel I contribute my share in realising our vision.
5. I am proud to work for my organisation.

B. Relations

1. I trust and feel at ease in our team.
2. I feel comfortable enough to give feedback (appreciation and adjustment) to colleagues.

3. I get feedback myself (both in appreciation and adjustment).

4. Team members do not shy away from confrontations, conflicts are resolved and used as learning experiences.

5. We keep relationships between team members optimal.

II. Autonomy

C. Guidance

1. All employees or trainees get the right support at the right time.

2. There is a good welcoming policy in our team.

3. There are clear rules, agreements and procedures to deal with concrete situations in my job.

4. The consultation periods are meaningful and efficient.

5. I receive sufficient material support to carry out my work efficiently.

D. Space

1. There is a clear framework, both substantive and organisational, within which I do my job.

2. This framework is sufficiently monitored.

3. I experience enough space to carry out my work my way.

4. I experience that, as a team, we have enough decision-making space to function together well

5. I experience that, as a team, we are sufficiently heard regarding decisions that affect us.

III. Competence

E. Roles

1. My talent and expertise are used to their full potential in our team.

2. The roles in our team are well-matched for the talent and expertise of each member.

3. My role in my team energises me.

4. The responsibilities regarding my role in the team are clear.

5. Tasks that offer no or less joy are shared equitably in the team.

F. Reflection

1. I receive the coaching I need.

2. At consultation moments, sufficient time is taken to reflect together.

3. Roles and their inclusion are adequately evaluated and adjusted.

4. There is plenty of room to learn, experiment and reflect.

5. I am offered sufficient development opportunities.

IV. Result

G. Result

1. The team result/ mission is clear.

2. My contribution to the team assignment is clear and sufficiently evaluated with me.

3. In our team, we do enough to seek improvement and quality.

4. My goals are ambitious but achievable.

5. Throughout the year, my goals and those of the team give me enough direction to set the right priorities.

CASE STUDY: SERVANT-LEADERSHIP AT ZOTTEGEM GENERAL HOSPITAL

This book might sound like a series of ideal scenarios. Of course, day-to-day reality is often a lot bumpier than what is depicted in a book. Yet servant-leadership aims precisely to make a difference in the daily practice of teams and organisations. In the concluding part of this book, I want to illustrate the potential power of servant-leadership. I do this in two ways.

First of all, I briefly outline a program on servant-leadership that I carried out at the General Hospital in Zottegem. It didn't involve just one team or a handful of managers, but the entire organisation, which reoriented itself around the principles, mental models and convictions highlighted in this book.

Finally, in the epilogue that follows, I answer some (perhaps intuitive) critical questions that this form of leadership may raise: isn't ser-vant-leadership too soft? Doesn't it only work for people who hardly need guidance? Isn't it at odds with the pyramidal structure of our organisation? How do you get an entire organisation moving around servant-leadership? I use these insights to show that there are indeed practical applications of the theory and that you will become stronger as a leader and as an organisation by putting servant-leadership principles into practice in your organisation.

General Hospital Zottegem has about a thousand employees. Their collective ambition is to offer high-quality care to their patients. The way to achieve this is by fully focusing on satisfied employees and robust teams. 'To get the best out of employees and teams in a sustainable way, we want to facilitate managers and enable them to use the maximum potential of our employees,' says Vanessa De Mulder, director of personnel and organisation of AZ Sint-Elisabeth. 'We want a leadership style that allows this and that is adapted to the needs of the organisation, of the employees and of the leaders themselves. We also want to meet a number of challenges facing our organisation and act from a shared vision of leadership. In short, we as an HR team aim for an efficient, effective, sustainable and integral approach in developing our employee and leadership policy.'

Vanessa testifies: 'The leadership process went through several phases. First, with our eight-member management team, we pondered the role of the leader: how would we like to be managed ourselves? What kind of leadership gets the best out of our employees? What is our vision for leadership? What is the situation now and where do we want to go? What are the practical and financial implications? Where is the yardstick and what support are we willing to provide as an organisation?

This created the preconditions for the **strategic vision of leadership** needed to implement the principles of servant-leadership in the hospital. The conclusion was that in order for all leaders in the hospital to develop into servant-leaders, some fundamental and optional choices would have to be made. Questions about the interpretation of roles, tasks of the manager and the adaptation of existing job profiles were on the table.

In the spirit of servant-leadership, we organised a **kick-off with all 50 executives.** There, they fleshed out the vision of leadership in concrete terms. Together, for instance, they found out that they were often doing up to 90 per cent of their colleagues' work. Like them, they also did weekend shifts, operational tasks and were the point of contact for colleagues inside and outside the team. Yet both the organisation and the employees expected a more strategic role from managers. Feedback was often missed; people did not always feel connected to the service, targets were not set, people were not used to their maximum potential and time was lost to duplication of work or things that were perceived as inefficient.

There was a brainstorming session on what the managers could undertake from the three roles. In turn, the teams were allowed to consider the question: what do you need from your manager in order to stay fully motivated?

This was followed by a **three-day learning programme** on servant-leadership in groups of about ten managers: a day on the role of manager, the role of leader and the role of coach. This allowed the managers to deal with all practical questions; they were trained in conversation management; they could experiment with all kinds of methods and concrete tools to increase the autonomy, commitment and competence of employees together. According to Vanessa, it was "a constructive, connecting, enjoyable experience that also strengthened the bond between the executives."

Following this, the leaders redesigned their own roles and functions. Based on their shared vision of leadership, they drew up their own **job profiles**. They decided to focus on reducing their operational tasks and take on numerous responsibilities and mandates. This gave the teams the mandate and autonomy to select new employees themselves and gave them a full view of the working resources available to their departments. The managers' task now became primarily to work with their teams to seek out process improvements, optimise patient care, coach employees, train new employees, innovate by implementing new ideas, coordinate with other departments and monitor the hospital's policy. All this, of course, in a phased process, because each new task brings the challenge of an operational change, refocusing in a structured manner and seeking solutions for this within the teams if need be.

But how can we communicate all this to our employees and do so in an engaging, understandable and approachable way? A **video** explaining the essence of servant-leadership was made to support managers in explaining the principles to their teams.

Performance appraisals were also introduced for the first time. The job profile was used as a framework for this. The interview itself was prepared by managers and employees using the hand method, in order to arrive at SMART agreements. HR recorded these agreements in a procedure and supported the managers by making a handsome template for preparing the interviews.

Because all these changes caused some learning stress among the managers, the possibility of **individual coaching** was offered. A questionnaire (talent and motivation analysis) with a follow-up interview helped the managers gain insight into their own motives, talents and skills that might need to be developed. Their personal learning questions were also addressed.

As the executives together laid down their own yardstick, they chose not to let this be an optional exercise. Thus, a questionnaire was designed together with employees and executives to gauge the effects of servant-leadership within the broader context of an **engagement measurement**. To gauge the impact of leadership, the questions to employees were designed around the three roles of the leader.

For the position of head nurse, these are some preferred roles:
- My head nurse as manager:

  + My head nurse ensures that the tasks of the team members in my department are coordinated.

  + My head nurse ensures that work instructions are clear and uniform.

- My head nurse as leader:

  + My head nurse takes concrete initiatives to optimise interpersonal relationships between team members.

  + My head nurse ensures that the hospital's vision lives on in our team.

- My head nurse as a coach:

    + My head nurse provides adequate guidance
      in carrying out my work.

    + My head nurse makes enough time for consultation and feedback.

The process ended with a **team-building day**. It was decided to build in **annual supervision periods**, to permanently facilitate the managers in their renewed role and help them increase their autonomy not only on paper, but also in practice, in a feasible, pragmatic way, mindful of the culture and uniqueness of the organisation.

More information on this and other cases (video, images, presentations and all tools and templates used) can be found at
www.servant-leadership.world

EPILOGUE

When you examine this book with those around you or with your own critical mind, there are likely to be some questions that arise. For the most common ones, I provide answers below.

ISN'T SERVANT-LEADERSHIP TOO SOFT? DOESN'T IT ONLY WORK FOR PEOPLE WHO HARDLY NEED GUIDANCE?

Although servant-leadership promotes such concepts and behaviours as modesty, authenticity, honesty, trust and service, it is based on leadership. Everything starts with living up to the vision; that is why this comes first. The two pillars, the yardstick and the support, are about balancing expectations and the support we provide to achieve the collective ambition. So everything starts with the vision and the yardstick, and is indeed about being tough on those two things to get results.

Moreover, no one would choose 'soft leadership' just because it is soft and no one would choose 'hard leadership' just because it is hard. What every leader is looking for is effectiveness. The premise that the best long-term results are achieved with authoritarian leadership has been refuted several times. Servant-leadership is just as insistent on results as authoritarian leadership, only it starts from the knowledge that employees do not perform better in a threatening atmosphere where punishments and precepts are paramount. People, and therefore your organisation, flourish when everyone is given freedom, feels comfortable and is properly called to account when they fail to meet the yardstick.

ISN'T SERVANT-LEADERSHIP AT ODDS WITH THE PYRAMIDAL STRUCTURE OF OUR ORGANISATION?

On the contrary. The possible undesirable effects of the pyramid, such as an explicit power relationship, lack of trust or the absence of a feedback culture, often do not contribute at all to the quality of the product or service. Servant or facilitator leadership can overcome these undesirable effects of the pyramid and turn them into a flatter concentric circle organisational model. With servant-leadership, you choose to put your product or service back at the centre and surround yourself with it.

However, the reality is that the 'top executives' sometimes display dominant or authoritarian behaviour, appropriating huge benefits or salary increases for themselves while cutting the salaries of executive employees, and so on. Here, the organisation needs to examine the indirect effects (on motivation, costs, efficiency), develop a vision of leadership and define a yardstick around this together with the executives. In this way, desired behaviour can be rewarded and executives can be challenged if they perform below the yardstick.

HOW DO YOU GET AN ENTIRE ORGANISATION MOVING AROUND SERVANT-LEADERSHIP? IS A SERVANT-LEADERSHIP TRAINING COURSE THE SOLUTION?

Not necessarily! I advocate an integrated approach to leadership development in organisations. The traditional approach of training and education has some value, though in my view it is too limited. Managers are often very enthusiastic about the experiences and insights gained after training. Full of confidence, they then go back to the workplace. They return to their own organisation and its culture, with its own formal and informal reward systems, work processes, procedures, job maps and agreements that have been long established, as well as the same people with the same habits and patterns. The reaction is often: 'I do notice that those things play a role in the background in what I do' or 'I had so many good intentions, but unfortunately I haven't really had the time to realise them'. A practical example like the one described in the Case Study on Servant-Leadership is precisely about initiating an overall, structural reform. Only then can training have a lasting and major impact.

WHEN DOES A LEADERSHIP PROGRAMME HAVE THE MAXIMUM CHANCE OF SUCCESS?

If the return on investment in learning programmes around leadership is not very high, we are missing something. After all, enough time, money and energy are put into it to raise the bar a little higher. My hypothesis is that the influence of the environment on leadership behaviour is underestimated and the training and education effort lacks the right framework conditions to achieve behavioural change. Also, some managers lack certain talents. They will prove most effective if they seek solutions for the skills they lack from within the team to make up for their deficiencies. Thus, a team leader without a talent for coaching can still become a good coach within or outside the team.

The influence on the organisational environment can be great, but you can only influence it if you work with your organisation as a whole. In this way, you can make servant-leadership permeate all facets of the organisation. Experience shows that it is often only then that we see real change on the shop floor. Here are some recommendations on how to create an environment in which servant-leadership can be incorporated:

- Establish a vision for leadership with your employees and managers. Start from the simple question: which form of leadership (behaviour and characteristics) in our team leads to happy employees and sustainable results? Summarise the vision briefly and robustly, and make it visible throughout the organisation.

- You can redesign your organisation's governance or test it against this vision. Should mandates become formalized in the organisation? Make sure that not too much power or mandates come together in a single person.

- Decentralise your policies as much as possible, and be transparent about the information available. Give disclosure to managers about the number of full-time equivalent workers, the training budget, and so on.

- Get management to visit the teams every quarter to hear how everything is going as part of your organisation's policy. The teams can then tell which achievements they are most proud of, what innovative ideas they have come up with, what obstacles they found in their work or what could help them do their job even better.

- For example, let each manager take charge of the hiring of new employees. Let the employees themselves choose which of them will lead their team. If necessary, lay this down in a procedure.

- Together with managers, prioritise what their main tasks are and where they can free up time to take up their role as servant-leaders (see quadrant 2 - not urgent, but important - on p.[xxx]).

- Set the yardstick for managers from this vision: what are the result areas and tasks? What are the most important skills, with which associated behaviours? Let this come up daily, as well as during regular formal conversations.

- On this basis, question employees about the performance of their leaders. Have employees evaluate the quality of leadership they receive. After all, their experiences are the ultimate test of leadership development. Be assertive on behaviour of leaders that is below par. This is absolutely critical to making a lasting culture shift.

Keep in mind that the above adjustments often have to be approved by those in a position of power. The challenge is to anticipate that those people will not want to give up their privileged position without a fight. This requires personal leadership to act on your own values, commitment to the collective ambition and a choice for the organisation as a whole.

AND WHAT IF OUR ORGANISATION IS NOT YET READY FOR THIS?

In recent years, we have guided many organisations in implementing servant-leadership. In the beginning, we did so mainly with inspirational learning processes. But honestly, that did not always turn out to be the ideal approach. Indeed, sometimes there is work to be done with the organisation itself.

ORGANIZATION & TEAMS IN 'DRIVE'

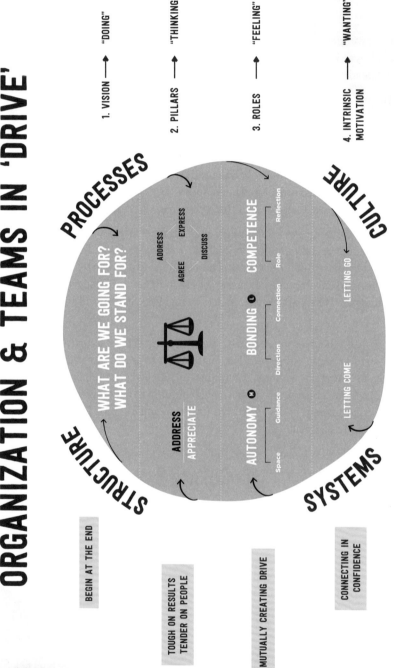

PROCESSES

CULTURE

STRUCTURE

SYSTEMS

WHAT ARE WE GOING FOR?
WHAT DO WE STAND FOR?

ADDRESS
EXPRESS
AGREE
DISCUSS

COMPETENCE
Role
Reflection

BONDING
Connection

AUTONOMY
Guidance
Direction

ADDRESS
APPRECIATE

Space

LETTING GO

LETTING COME

1. VISION ⟶ "DOING"

2. PILLARS ⟶ "THINKING"

3. ROLES ⟶ "FEELING"

4. INTRINSIC MOTIVATION ⟶ "WANTING"

BEGIN AT THE END

TOUGH ON RESULTS
TENDER ON PEOPLE

MUTUALLY CREATING DRIVE

CONNECTING IN CONFIDENCE

After all, the team operates within a broader context, and that context has a major impact on what the team can achieve. If that context does not serve a team's drive, the effect of training is often short-lived. After all, every day the team is influenced by the organisation's strategy, structure, culture, processes and systems. You can see this clearly in the diagram on page 226.

For example, the other day we were at a company where an administrative assistant was told to submit an application for... a stapler. Because of the cumbersome structure, red tape, slow processes and outdated systems, it took no less than two months for him to get approval for something he would simply pick up from the shop at home.

This led me to write a new book: "Respond!" In it, I describe a step-by-step method to reinvent your organisation, based on the foundations of connection, trust and shared responsibility. If you take this journey, you can arrive at a responsive organisation. In it, self-organisation, co-creation and wholeness will be central. Let us briefly explain these concepts:

Self-organisation: where you not only allow the greatest possible autonomy in the execution of the job, but also responsibility for organising the whole thing. The team not only has a meadow with fence posts within which it can act autonomously, it also decides where the posts are located and can move them if necessary.

Co-creative goals: where organisation, teams, employees and clients go for it together. This starts from a firm commitment to the vision, and immediately transcends it. We are constantly in touch with our situation to make policy together and adjust it where necessary.

Wholeness: choosing to look beyond a person's competences. The employee is viewed with confidence in his or her totality. In our experience, an organisation built from these three building blocks creates the ideal environment for teams and employees with drive.

IN CONCLUSION

To write this book, I linked my experiences in the workplace to existing models and wrote down my personal impressions in the process. However, this can never be more than a snapshot in time. All systems evolve; a human being is not a static entity and life is a constant adaptation to new situations.

Robert Greenleaf, founder of servant-leadership, said the following about an organisation's raison d'être: 'The organisation exists to provide meaningful work to the employee as well as to provide a product or service to the customer.' In my view, it is important that employees are not only viewed as a 'means' to pursue worthwhile ambitions, but also as an end in themselves. Let's strive to give employees far-reaching autonomy, in an appreciative learning climate, where they are empowered, feel connected to a meaningful cause and achieve great things. In this way, together we will not only go for more satisfaction and better results in our work, but also for more people living happy lives.

TAKING CONTROL OF YOUR OWN LEARNING!

We are often asked what the next concrete steps are to further develop servant-leadership skills. We like to suggest four possibilities:

- Sign up for a Servant-Leadership Masterclass: an in-depth learning experience to enhance your vision and skills.
- Invite us to your organisation: We can facilitate a hands-on learning programme with you and your colleagues. It can be in English, French or Dutch.
- Discover the book 'Respond!' If you want to know more about creating the right context for servant-leadership in your organisation, I recommend reading my book 'Respond!'. You can download the first part of the book and find a free questionnaire on our website: dienendleidinggeven.be/respond.
- Make your organisation responsive. Together with your colleagues, why not give the organisation a makeover? Focus on self-organisation, co-creation and wholeness as building blocks for the ideal environment in which teams can flourish and servant-leadership can flourish.

I wish you all much surrender, gentleness towards yourself and flow in your development as human beings and leaders!

For more information or a completely free consultation:

www.servant-leadership.world

ACKNOWLEDGEMENTS

I did not write this book alone. Over the past ten years, about a thousand executives have helped shape this thinking. They challenged me to make the frameworks more concrete and provided the inspiration for this book.

Thank you to my colleagues Bram, Lori, Tako and Tom from Roedel Consult. Thank you for being such spirited companions. What a blessing to be able to work with you.

Special thanks to Bram Kelchtermans for taking this thinking into the world with such confidence and fire. I cannot imagine a better ambassador.

Thank you to Jef. For your incredible writing talent and the fun together while writing. Merci for taking this book to the next level.

Furthermore, my special thanks go to the professionals of Tripleclick Design and Lannoo Campus. Thank you for your continued commitment and brilliant work.

Thank you to my dear mother. You were for me the living example of a servant leader and thus a great inspiration for this book. You still inspire me daily. I dedicate this book to you with all my heart.

Thanks to the Source of life itself. For your support and love. Thank You that we may experience life in all its fullness. Thank you for always being there.

Proceeds from this book will go to Faja Lobi, a reforestation project in Congo.

Any comments or suggestions about the book are welcome. They can be integrated into the next edition.
Feel free to email roeland@roedelconsult.be.

LITERATURE

- Bellens, K., Davidson T., Delcour F. & De Stobbeleir K. (2012). The Learning Guide, Towards a positive learning climate in organisations. Ghent: Vlerick Leuven Gent Management School.

- Boyatzis, R.E. (2006). An Overview of Intentional Change From a Complexity Perspective. Journal of Management Development, 25(7).

- Buckingham, M. (2012). Discovering your strengths. Houten: Spectrum.

- Clement, J. (2008). Inspiring Coaching. Leuven: LannooCampus/Scriptum.

- Collins, J. (2001). Good to great. New York: Harper Business.

- Covey, S. (1989). The Seven Habits of Highly Effective Leaders. Amsterdam: Business Contact.

- Csikszentmihalyi, M. (2007). Flow. Psychology of optimal experience. Amsterdam: Boom.

- Dale, E. (1954). Audio-visual methods in teaching. New York: The Dryden Press.

- Decuyper, S., Dochy, F. & Van den Bossche, P. (2010). Team learning. The key to effective teamwork. Leuven: KU Leuven.

- De Rick, K., Van Valckenborgh, K. & Baert, H. (2004). A conceptual framework for the operationalisation of the term 'learning climate'. Leuven: KU Leuven.

- Dewulf, L. (2012). I choose my talent. Leuven: LannooCampus/ Scriptum.

- Dilts, R. (2008). Coaching from a multifaceted perspective. Heemskerk: Andromeda.

- Effectory & Intermediair. (s.d.). The largest and most reliable list of the best workplaces in the Netherlands. Accessed 12-08-2016 via (https://www.beste-werkgevers.nl).

- Gill, L. (2000). Collaborating with anyone. Even with your partner. Houten: Spectrum.

- Gordon, T. (2010). Effective Leadership. Antwerp: Kosmos.

- Greenleaf, R. (2003). The Servant-Leader within. A transformative path. New Jersey: Paulist Press.

- Hersey, P. & Blanchard, K.H. (1977). Management of Organizational Behavior: Utilizing Human Resources. (3rd ed.) New Jersey, Prentice Hall.

- Hersey, P. (2014). Situational Leadership. Amsterdam: Business Contact.

- IJzermans, T. (2009). Bears on the road, spins in your head. Zaltbommel: Thema.

- Judge, T., et al (2010). The relationship between pay and job satisfaction: A meta-analysis of the literature. Journal of vocational behaviour, 77, 157-167.

- Karssing, E. (2006). Integrity in professional practice. Assen: Van Gorcum.

- Laloux, F. (2015) Reinventing Organizatons. Leuven: LannooCampus.

- Nuijten, I. (2011). Serving true leaders. The Hague: Academic Service.

- Ofman, D. (2015). Inspiration and quality in oganisations. Utrecht: Servire.

- Packard, J. in Mech, D. & Boitani L. (2003). Wolves: behaviour, ecology and conservation. Chicago: University of Chicago Press.

- Pink, D. (2013). Drive. Amsterdam: Business Contact.

- Rath, T. & Conchie, B. (2008). Strengths-based leadership.
  New York: Gallup Press.

- Reddin, W. (1989). The Smart Manager's Book of Lists.
  Cleveland: Lake Publishing Company.

- Rosenberg, M. (2011). Nonviolent communication.
  Rotterdam: Lemniscaat.

- Semler, R. (2013). Semco style. Amsterdam: The Bookstore.

- Stewart, I. & Joines, V. (2010). Transactional Analysis; The
  handbook for personal and professional use.
  Amsterdam: SWP.

- Tellegen, T. (1993). Almost everyone could fall over.
  Amsterdam: Querido.

- Ten Hoedt, F., Tuckman, B.W. & Jensen, M.A.C. (1977). Stages of
  Small Group development revisited.
  London, Group Organisation Studies, International Authors.

- Van Amelsvoort, G. & Van Jaarsveld, J. (2000) Team
  development and leadership. Vlijmen: ST-Groep.

- Van Damme, C. (2003). Coaching team leadership.
  Unpublished VOCA text.

- Vandendriessche, F. & Clement, J. (2006). Leading without orders.
  Leuven: LannooCampus/Scriptum.

- Vangronsveld, G. (2007). Power of a team.
  Leuven: LannooCampus/Scriptum.

- Vangronsveld, G. & Dewulf, L. (2012). Help, my batteries
  are running low! Leuven: LannooCampus/Scriptum.

- Van IJzendoorn, E., Van Weert, L. & Müller, B. (2015). Practice
  book From talent to performance. Utrecht: Ehrm Vision.

- Van Vugt, M. & Wildschut, M. (2012).
  Authority. Utrecht: Bruna Publishers.

- Whitmore, J. (2010). Successful coaching. Amsterdam: Nelissen.

- Van Vugt, M. & Wildschut, M. (2012).
  Gezag. Utrecht: Bruna Uitgeverij.

- Whitmore, J. (2010). Succesvol coachen. Amsterdam: Nelissen.

LEADERS ON SERVANT-LEADERSHIP

'The leader of the future is servant and subservient. First and foremost, he or she is loyal to the organisation's mission. His or her own agenda is secondary to it. A leader who "lives" his organisation's mission naturally finds long-term direction and strategy. With this book, Roeland provides a clear and useful model and proves that he is close to everyday practice.'

— Wouter Torfs
CEO Schoenen Torfs, voted Best Place To Work six times

'Servant-Leadership outlines a clear model and is peppered with telling examples. The author has an undeniable feel for practice.'

— Frank Van Massenhove
Chairman Belgian Federal Public Service Social Security, Government Manager of the Year 2007

'Our participatory society in which we are shifting from "caring for" to "caring that" cannot do without servant-leadership. This book offers fantastic practical tools for that. Highly recommended!'

— Dirk-Jan de Bruijn
Director The Innovation Centre

'Ik herken Roelands inspirerende stijl vanaf de eerste pagina tot de laatste. Met dit werk rond dienend leidinggeven schetst hij een helder model, boordevol sprekende voorbeelden en met een duidelijke voeling met de praktijk.'

— Koen Oosterlinck
Managing director Brothers of Charity (Partner in welfare, mental health and education)

'I experienced Servant-Leadership as a practical, instructive, useful *guide; a real workbook. It is full of useful (self)reflections, exercises, mnemonics, checklists and recommendations that put you as a reader in a learning and doing mode in an inviting and serving way.'*

— Dick Rochat
Executive coach, leadership expert and programme maker at the Greenleaf Center for Servant-Leadership Europe

'Servant-Leadership reads delightfully, speaks the language of executives, prompts thinking, inspires, motivates and is concrete in terms of translation and advice. Highly recommended for anyone who wants their team and organisation to shine naturally.'

— Monique van Elst
Manager at the Netherlands National Institute for Public Health and the Environment

'Servant-leadership is a practical guide to achieving one inspiring vision of leadership in your organisation. We now speak the same language. There is room to further develop our own leadership style from the same view on managing employees within an appreciative and caring personnel policy.'

— Jan Artois
Director Steevliet

'This is a book that many people in management positions can benefit from.'

— Prof Jaap Uijlenbroek
Director general of the State Property Agency

'With the practical tools provided in this book, I can do even better justice to the talents of our people.'

— Bastian Müller
Director TMA Method

'If employees within the organisation function well and the manager does not, the organisation can still continue to function well. The strength of the organisation is therefore mainly in the employees. Servant-leadership provides tools to let managers and employees perform optimally'.

— Toon Gerbrands
Director PSV Eindhoven

'For me, this book is the ultimate reflection tool. The frameworks formulated by Roeland help me in looking at my own practice. Because Roeland knows how to give clear words to them, this book also enables conversation about practice. Therein, I think, lies the true power of this work.'

— Bram Kelchtermans
Mooss asbl